THE COMPLETE POTTER:

ANIMAL FORMS AND FIGURES

1 Cat, height 13 cm (5 in). Roughly grogged clay with brush-painted raku glazes (Peter Crotty)

THE COMPLETE POTTER:

ANIMAL FORMS AND FIGURES

ROSEMARY WREN

SERIES EDITOR EMMANUEL COOPER

B.T. Batsford Ltd, London

To
W.A. ('Bill') Ismay M.B.E.
friend and collector of ceramics
whose delighted and minute awareness of difference
has sharpened the self-critical faculties
of a whole generation of potters

The front cover shows Australian Black
Swans, length 46 cm (18 in), made by
Rosemary Wren in stoneware, and painted
by Peter Crotty (1986). The Curled-up Cat
on the back cover is also of stoneware and
has a diameter of 24 cm (9½ in). Again this is
the work of Rosemary Wren and Peter
Crotty.

First published 1990

ISBN 0 7134 61276
Typeset by Servis Filmsetting Ltd,
Manchester

And printed in Hong Kong

For the publishers
B. T. Batsford Limited
4 Fitzhardinge Street
London W1H 0AH

CONTENTS

ACKNOWLEDGEMENTS

I am deeply grateful to the twelve other makers of sculptural ceramics who, without hesitation, have taken time off from their work to produce contributions which have enlivened not only this book but my own outlook. Their names appear appropriately. Anna Adams I thank especially for permission to use her poem 'Brother Fox'; and my partner, Peter Crotty, for his patience with my inevitable preoccupation and his perceptive comments on word-usage.

Photographs of our work from three private collections are included: Figs. 26, 28, 29, 30 and 34 are owned by Gladys and Harley Barnes; the swans on the front cover by Brian Bearne, and Fig. 38 by Anne and Adrian Hinkins. This expresses my appreciation of their encouragement as well as their helpfulness.

The Royal Albert Memorial Museum, Exeter, most kindly gave permission to photograph and reproduce Figs. 3, 6, 7 and 9; my thanks for permission to reproduce are also due to the Ashmolean Museum (Fig. 5), the Victoria and Albert Museum (Fig. 24), and the Cambridge University Press (Fig. 10). Fig. 72 is by K. and J. Jelley; Fig. 47 is from *Ceramic Review*.

Last – but by no means least – I thank Stephen Brayne for his sensitive recording of ceramic qualities. All the photographs of my own work are his, as well as Figs. 1, 12, 17, 21, 46, 49, 57, 65 and both the jacket illustrations.

BROTHER FOX

Men net the seeming-docile hills
   in mesh of walls, but fail
to kill the fox of the high fells
   who lives beyond the pale.

I trickle under drystone walls
   while staid law-keepers dream,
and creep, when mooncast shadow falls,
   towards the valley farm.

The serpent writhes in my backbone,
   the snake dances in yours,
and treacherously lets me in
   to snap my wanton jaws.

Men load the valley fields with walls
   but still cannot subdue
the bandit of the stony fells
   who lives, deep-earthed, in you.

I trot, blood-dark, close by the wall
   under snow-smothered moon,
printing bad news with each footfall
   towards the winking town.

The serpent writhes in my backbone,
   the snake dances in yours,
and hypnotises gentle men
   into bloodlust and wars.

Anna Adams

INTRODUCTION

Art or craft? Sculpture or ceramics? Potters or not? The objects in this book elude such classification; their makers inhabit the world of intuition, which is concerned with relating not separating. Artists they certainly are; acutely aware of other living beings, they have a compelling need to record them and their ways, translated through the medium of clay. This hard taskmaster can be relied upon to retaliate if mistreated; it demands craft skills and knowledge. Yet as skill develops it lures on with ever-greater challenges. Size is limited only by the available kiln. Colour, pattern, texture – all are part of the ceramic inheritance, defying the passage of time. Natural forms can retreat to become the stylized starting-point for formal juxtapositions enjoyed for their own sake – but these again develop emotional overtones that reflect back on their origins.

All this is open to those who accept the discipline of this most responsive of materials – far more, however, can be related to it. Much of the contemporary work shown is by potters whose experience of clay includes making wheel-thrown vessels. All of them draw, some paint – perhaps as an end

2 Bluetits, life-size. Pattern incised in clay, colours filled in with matt glazes (white, yellow, blue) and black cobalt oxide (RDW/PMC)

in itself, but the trained eye retains images and stores information for further use. One writes poetry; words can extend the ceramic theme or ceramics epitomize the words. Another coaxes music from clay forms. Historical references can be made, sociological themes followed, fantasy can be untrammelled . . . though at the moment it appears quite *avant-garde* simply to stand up for the natural world. Certainly a sense of the earth is inevitably present in our materials.

Sculptural ceramics indeed know no bounds. However, there are not so very many ways of making the essential hollow forms with which they are constructed. Here we show some paths through this possibly confusing maze, and the various ends to which they can lead. We hope that connoisseurs and critics may find this book enlightening, as well as potters seeking further scope for their own work.

1 SOURCES AND DEVELOPMENT OF IDEAS

The writer of any book for potters has to solve a proverbial chicken-and-egg situation: nothing can be made without ideas; ideas are formless without some knowledge of techniques; techniques demand understanding of materials; materials are chosen as the expression of an idea. So how can one ever get started at all?

The making of animals and people in clay is a means by which individuals can relate themselves to the historic past, to the earth and its forces, and to other living beings. Although ceramic form is often sculptural, the techniques in this book are not in general those of the sculptor, but are those of the potter whose interest is in the behaviour of clay and how it is affected by fire. This potter's sculpture, using the everyday pot-making methods of its time, is found everywhere. Museum visits are an excellent way of developing an awareness of the wide range of historical precedents.

Very little, however, is gained by just looking and passing on. As your intention is to build up a rich mental store of source material, photography is not sufficiently probing. The only real way to look is by making a drawing. You may think you have seen, but in order to draw it is necessary to keep your brain at full stretch, making a whole series of decisions; you become aware of unsuspected aspects and emotional overtones. It matters not one jot whether the marks on the paper might be considered good or bad by others; you are not setting out to make a complete description for them. This kind of drawing is very personal, a visual conversation with yourself. Even if you have never attempted to draw before, it will open the doors of insight in your mind, telling you where your own interest lay in that particular object, and which were the outstanding characteristics. These will inevitably be different for each person according to their previous experience, thus gradually ensuring that your drawings take on a personal style. I am often surprised by my own drawings, for the process is largely unconscious.

A small pocket sketchbook is ideal – it is unobtrusive and discourages people from peering over your shoulder to observe such a remarkable occupation in action. Stiff covers are essential. It may not be cheap, but you

3 and 4 (overleaf) Mounted Warrior, height 17 cm (6¾ in), Cycladic Islands. Late period (Royal Albert Memorial Museum, Exeter)

will be referring to it and its successors for the rest of your working life. Carry it everywhere, and visit the ethnographical section of every museum, large or small, wherever you are.

Eventually you will find yourself able to see living animals and people with the same eyes outside the museum; but don't just think you can remember – *draw* them. These are the drawings that can be used again and

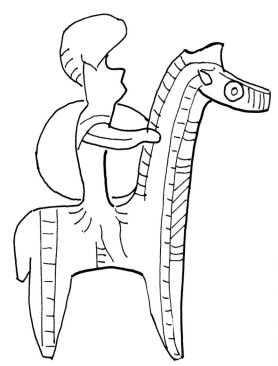

again as the foundation of your own work. Clay objects made directly from them will have your own personal stamp, soundly based on traditional experience.

Look back through your sketchbook thinking to yourself 'Why did I choose to draw this object rather than another?'. Some animal forms and figures – such as the Cycladic *Mounted Warrior* in Fig. 3 – have more life than others: how does this come about? Here lies the most important question, to which the answer is elusive and inevitably paradoxical. It is entirely to do with the makers' attitude of mind: the more realistic their intentions, the less real the result. Copies are inevitably lifeless, whether of living creatures or other objects. A work of art exists in its own right; its creator needs reverence for life combined with respect for materials. Success comes from the resolution of these two apparent incompatibles. Reverence for life (to quote Bertrand Russell) means feeling 'in all that lives . . . something individual and strangely precious, the growing principle of life, an embodied fragment of the dumb striving of the world'.

This is shown supremely well in the Kathakali dance of Kerala in south India. The dancer is thinking himself into being, in rapid sequence, not only a deity or another human being but an elephant in the jungle, majestically waving his ears, pulling up a tussock of grass with his trunk, and knocking off the earth before tucking it neatly into his mouth; then the tiger, his eye-

muscles contracting and quivering in the same way as those of a domestic cat sighting prey. The 'materials' are the dance and its symbolism, given ephemeral existence by the dancer's body; ours is clay – soft and malleable until given endless endurance by fire. The Indian dancer in his ritually-formalized attire by no means looks like an elephant or a tiger; neither need our clay object be like the creature of flesh and blood, fur or feathers that inspired it. The mysterious alchemy is the empathy in the mind of the artist, carried out with absolute respect for the 'clay way' – the fundamental qualities to be found in the nature of the material as the form and structure of the work develop, in the same way as the rhythm and structure of the dance.

The clay humans, animals, and birds shown in Figs. 3–10 and 12 have been chosen to show some of the traditional ways in which this problem has been solved. How can they help you? My suggestion is that a basic vocabulary could be acquired by first making careful studies of them all in clay, and then making another series, using the same methods but with different animals and people of your own. As a further step to develop courage and a sense of scale, make your own again, but two or three times the size; new solutions will evolve as you work on the new problems that arise.

Other methods of constructing clay sculpture can be found in Haniwa, coiled figures from ancient Japanese tombs; in the

5 Zebu vessel, handbuilt. From Amlach in the Caucasus. 8th–10th century BC (Ashmolean Museum, Oxford)

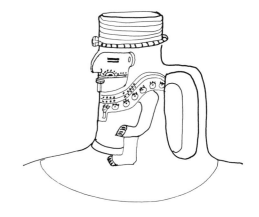

7, 8 Jar-neck figure, height 15 cm (6 in), Quimbaya style, Middle Cauca Valley, Columbia (RAMM, Exeter)

6 Two figures, height 14 cm and 16 cm ($5\frac{1}{2}$ and $6\frac{1}{2}$ in). Press-moulded Moche pottery, pre-Columbian Peru (RAMM, Exeter)

thrown saltglaze of La Borne, to be seen at Bourges in central France; in Etruscan canopic urns and life-size tomb figures, Chinese dancers of the Han dynasty, and Indian votive figures. Look out for this quality of life in other materials too: Julebok goats of straw from Scandinavia carrying the harvest from one year to the next; American Indian totems carved in wood holding the strength of tribal identity; Eskimo stonecarving; ancient Mediterranean bronzes; Javanese shadow puppets of pierced buffalo hide; symbolic cloisonné enamels from China, and the painted creatures of imagination that illuminate Celtic manuscripts. None of these bears any superficial realistic resemblance to living animals or humans, but each holds their essence, instantly recognizable, expressed through the qualities of their materials. Draw all these or others like them, noticing how the natural form has been adapted (*Fig. 11*), and then see how they would work out in clay. This two-stage adaptation is a very useful exercise for escaping from the trammels of realism.

Our problem today is that all these things were made to focus spiritual power; as commerce creeps in, the power evaporates. We may not now see the natural phenomena with which we are surrounded as dwellings for powerful spirits ruling our existence, but given reverence for life we can still celebrate its diverse manifestations. The symbolic reasons for bringing young bulls down from

9 Duck vessel, height 12 cm (4¾ in) coiled. American Indian, 19th century. South-western States of America (RAMM, Exeter)

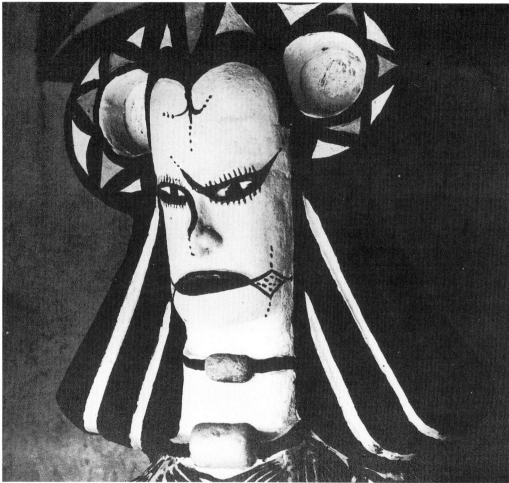

10 Ala the Earth Goddess, from an Ibo Mbari House, West Africa. Larger than human size (From African Mud Sculpture *by Ulli Beier, Cambridge University Press, 1963)*

the mountains to run loose in small Peruvian towns may be lost, but the snorting wild masculinity of their traditional clay representations is unmistakable (*Fig. 12*).

When I was first feeling my way towards making handbuilt animals (having made pots for some years before being introduced to the technique which is described in chapter 4) I began with this type of museum study. Discovering from this that attempts to make a realistic likeness were not only unnecessary but a pitfall to be avoided at all costs, it then seemed that drawing from life would be the wrong path: my own feeling would be what mattered. Adaptations from the past were helpful exercises but led to a dead end: the approach of their makers was no longer possible. I needed to find a means of development that would release my creative springs of originality.

A sense of freedom being the first essential, I bought large inexpensive layout pads containing many sheets of thin crisp paper. Stiff covers were not necessary as they were not for carrying around. Delving inwards, I drew simplified shapes of creatures as they came into my mind; and then, keeping the same underlying abstract geometry, I made dozens of variations, stretching them outwards or upwards as in a distorting mirror. Some of these free little drawings are reproduced here to show the idea (*Fig. 13*) with resulting *Pigeons* (*Fig. 15*).

This is an excellent loosening-up exercise, and one series can produce enough for many

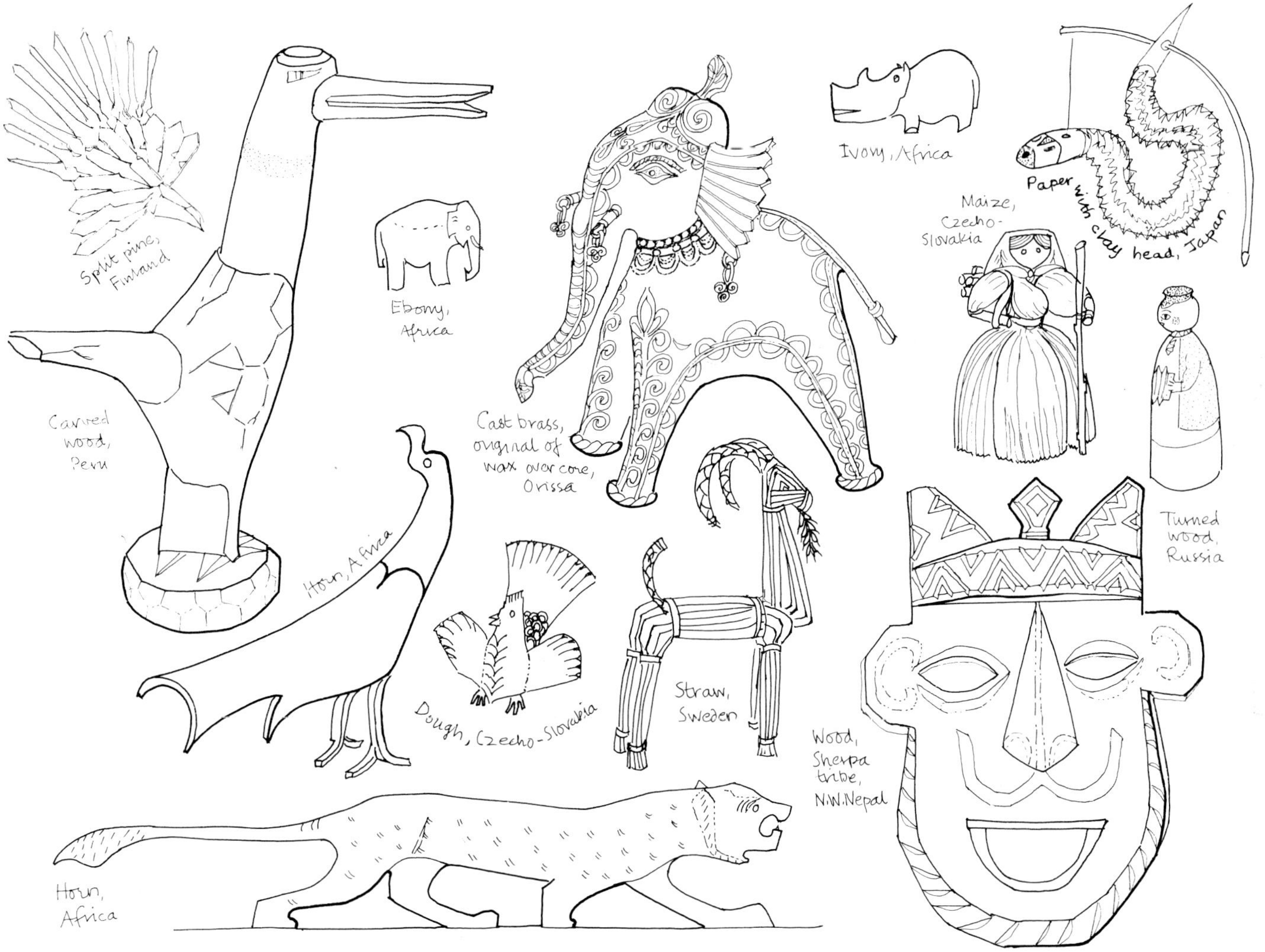
Split pine, Finland
Carved wood, Peru
Ebony, Africa
Cast brass, original of wax over core, Orissa
Ivory, Africa
Maize, Czecho-Slovakia
Paper with clay head, Japan
Horn, Africa
Dough, Czecho-Slovakia
Straw, Sweden
Turned wood, Russia
Wood, Sherpa tribe, N.W. Nepal
Horn, Africa

11 *Adaptation of natural forms to various materials (author's collection)*

12 Ceremonial Bull, length 36 cm
(14 in), traditional, Peru (author's
collection)

13 Mind-stretching drawings (RDW)

weeks' work, each piece turning out to be quite different in character: fat or thin, restful or tense, contemplative or alert. Such is the power of the abstract qualities of form.

I remember being told as a student that Michelangelo's painting of the Hand of God on the ceiling of the Sistine Chapel owes its ability to single each person out for its message not to the superb draughtsmanship but to its dart-like overall shape. My simple drawings were deliberately two-dimensional, stating that this part of the profile was to be so long in relation to that, meeting at such-and-such an angle. They were largely drawn in straight lines to clarify this – a very useful tool. The third dimension could then be

found in the making, avoiding the mere copying of something predetermined. It also allowed for wide interpretation, for a surface indicated by a vertical line could well belong to a form that leaned sharply towards you or equally away, or any point in between. This helps one to develop the ability to visualize and compare shapes and patterns in the mind's eye. The reply to the question 'But how does one know which is the right answer?' can only be 'It looks right'. One's mind goes quiet – alternatives cease to present themselves. It is necessary to have faith in this entirely intuitive process and then to proceed with determination.

I had been making handbuilt animals for

some years before I was able to see living creatures in terms of my particular sort of clay forms. It came about through the reconstruction of the garden outside my window. I was digging away a bank to lower the general level and decided to ease the effort of shifting soil by heaping some of it up into a brick-walled mound about 1.5m (5ft) across, with a flat top level with the window-ledge. This made an excellent bird-table (needless to say we had no cats in those days). The intention was to see the birds at eye-level so as to be able to envisage them in clay, and it worked admirably. I spent enjoyable hours with my large-size sketch pad, spread out comfortably on the table

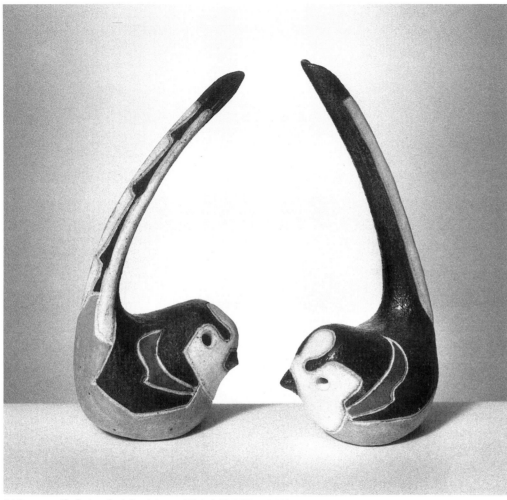

14 Long-tailed tits, height 14 cm (5½ in) (RDW, 1988)

indoors whatever the weather, finding the simplest answers to the question 'Now, how do I know that this one is a blue-tit and that is a robin?' – if necessary consulting a bird book. There was also the question of plumage and colour and how to deal with them in pottery terms, keeping to the limitations of my everyday pot-making materials and methods. With the birds going about their own affairs in front of me, happily feeding and establishing their pecking order without interruption, there was time to think all this out.

Watching them move, turning their heads to look at each other, or keeping a wary eye out for danger, taught me to see the varying articulation of different species. Some can turn their heads round further than others; some have to lean over to look back; others turn their heads only. How does the head fit onto the shoulders? What was to be done about beaks that would be spiky and breakable in clay? Tails come in many shapes – broad, long and thin, upright and jaunty. Some birds raise their tails on landing, the extraordinary construction of feathers making a springing curve. The point of balance in a clay bird would be different, but perhaps this could be used to allow for long tails without tipping over (*Fig. 14*). The biggest problem of all, of course, is presented by their thin legs, which are totally impossible in clay. My solutions are shown in the photographs in chapters 4 and 5.

Perhaps I should mention that my mother

15 Pigeons, *height 20 cm (8 in) hollow, handbuilt. Saltglazed stoneware (RDW, 1958)*

had bred Australian parakeets in large outdoor aviaries, so there had always been birds in my life and although I was always conscious of their behaviour, I had never deliberately studied them in this way before. Likewise there were always animal friends in the family, and I had worked on farms and at Chessington Zoo and Circus, which all helped.

The bird-table drawings continued the conventionalized simplification of the earlier series, though they became somewhat more three-dimensional, as can be seen in Fig. 16. By this means one can search for the order underlying the myriad small differences of natural form and pattern without becoming confused; it is then easy to rebuild on the same basis again and again – as in music. It also imparts a timeless quality to the work, a feeling that the importance of the individual lies in its being representative of its race. Many people will say 'That's just like my cat!' or, better still, 'I never looked at sparrows until I bought yours – and now they all look like it!', and you will have struck a small blow for the greater appreciation of the natural world – a blow against the arrogance of the human race, which so easily assumes that the only proper way to be is standing upright on only two of your feet, with eyes on the front of your face, no feathers, and only a few patches of fur, mindlessly ignoring the vast range of shapes and attributes that characterize those with an equal claim to their fair share of the world.

In this chapter I have described my own sources of inspiration, but today – when individuals are no longer tied to the tradition of their time and place – there are as many approaches as there are potters; those to be found in chapters 7, 8, and 9 are very different from mine.

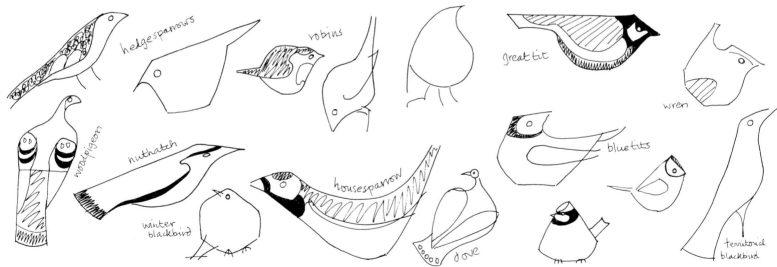

16 *Bird-table drawings (RDW)*

2 MATERIALS

It is going to be up to you to decide not only what to make, but also what to make it out of; this can appear to be a harrassing decision. Give it time to solve itself and keep other options open for the future.

Any clay that is good for making pots can, of course, be used for animal forms and figures made by potters' techniques, though some give more scope than others. It can be fine or rough, structurally strong or wayward and needing to be coaxed. Most importantly, it should hold itself up like a bridge, even in quite thin sections, whilst the clay is still plastic. Try out small quantities of different types – the feel of the clay under your fingers will tell you which one suits your temperament; this is what makes people become potters more than the appearance of the finished piece. I have worked my way through many different clays and firing temperatures, as can be seen in chapter 4. Continuing familiar themes but with the challenge of a new material is stimulating and not too drastic if the work starts to look bored.

You will feel the developing hollow forms strengthen or weaken as you find for yourself the principles of construction. Test different clays by rolling out long thin coils and standing them up as arches. The one that makes the tallest arch without collapsing will give you the most scope, though it could be that the interest of working with another overrides its disadvantages. Alter the texture to your liking by adding graded coarser materials; the safest are pre-fired clays such as grog made from fireclay, or molochite from China clay.

In this book we will not be considering methods foreign to normal studio potters' usage, such as making weak shapes that need extensive propping up, or solid forms that must be hollowed out before firing to avoid blowing up. Traditional sculptors use clay quite differently, as a means to an end rather than in its own right. They rely on an interior supporting armature of wires and rods that would make the piece impossible to dry without cracking, let alone to fire. Their eventual finished work is a copy of the surface modelling cast first in plaster, then in a quite different material such as bronze, after which the clay original is discarded. Our techniques accept the demands of the material more directly, using its limitations as the basis of our aesthetic.

My own interest is in the extraordinary structural strength of plastic clay. Having been first a throwing potter, all my animals and birds are basically pot-shaped, but many other types of structure making use of self-supporting skins have influenced them: the wonderfully delicate webs of the house-spider slung in the corners of the workshop window; the cells carefully modelled by honeybees out of wax to contain their brood and stores; the membranes of leaves; the interlocking barbs of feathers; shells of snails and sea creatures, and the chitin carapaces of beetles.

Exciting exploratory structures were being made by civil engineers and architects in reinforced concrete when modern structural analysis was new: such as Maillart's bridges in France, and Oscar Niemeyer's sculptural buildings for the new town of Brasilia in South America. By intensive calculation, they were pared down to use only the essential material demanded by the stresses and strains presented, producing objects of great elegance. The geodesic domes of Buckminster

Fuller in the United States taught me to emphasize diamond or triangular facets that appear in the course of construction on otherwise rather nebulous rounded forms; this imparts visual clarity and quite extraordinary structural strength. It is helpful to think of hollow clay structures as if you were small enough to stand inside them – they become the angular arched vaulting of Gothic cathedrals or the richly-rounded domes of Islamic mosques.

To this end I have sought out clays with exceptional green (i.e. unfired) strength. Strongest of all, and used by many famous potters, is 'T-material', mixed to a standardized formula and available from many suppliers in Britain and elsewhere (see Suppliers, p. 95). It is worth the very considerable extra expense, being absolutely reliable, minimizing losses from cracking or distortion, and holding its shape even above stoneware temperatures. Its qualities may well be due to a wetting agent that allows the particles to move closer together than usual, so that it remains plastic with less water. Otherwise it appears to be a ball clay with molochite grog. Treat it as a grogged stoneware clay and you won't go far wrong – but be wary of the way it quickly becomes too stiff to work.

In fact I find that T-material alone makes shapes that are visually too hard for my liking, so I mix it half-and-half with another clay. This could be done with any clay or mixed body from the vast range of different types on the shelves of the potters' suppliers. Detailed information on colour, texture, suitability for various uses, and firing temperatures are given in their catalogues; most are available plastic and ready for use.

Larger quantities are very much cheaper per kilo. As a guide to the amount likely to be required let me detail my own experience. We are two people working full time, one making and the other decorating, using a very labour-intensive technique of hand-building and brush-painting. Our pieces average 23 cm (9 in) long, each taking a day to make and a day to decorate, though many are smaller and a few much larger. In a year we get through (very roughly) 500 kg (half a ton) of mixed body. It is therefore worth buying 1000 kg (a ton) of T-material every four years or so. It comes in sealed plastic bags, making a stack of about 0.3 cu. m (12 cu ft), and improves in condition as time passes, providing it is protected from frost.

We also prefer to buy our clay direct from the pit. There are many reasons for this preference – in practical terms it is cheaper, there is more variety of choice, you know what you are using and where it comes from. But the deeper reason is the sense of continuity, reaching back to the origins of the Earth. It happens that we now live in south-west England, only a short distance from the Bovey Basin, an area 16 km by 6.5 km wide (10 miles by 4 miles) where enormous deposits of the finest potters' clay are mined. Anyone can see the huge pits between Chudleigh Knighton and Kingsteignton, north of Newton Abbot in Devonshire; beside the road are great open sheds with many compartments for clays of different colours and types, the lenticular strata being carefully kept separate by the operators using precisely controllable mechanical diggers. It is known as ball clay because it was previously dug out with special spades in blocks of regular size, known as balls.

Looking down into the pits, it fills one with awe to realize that the clay that filled up this primaeval lake – in places it is 1300 m (4000 ft) thick – has been lying there since it was washed down from its place of origin amongst the nearby heights of Dartmoor in torrential rainstorms between 50 and 35 million years ago. Even more awesome, as one attempts to have some appreciation of the lengths of geological time, is the fact that the granite of Dartmoor was formed between 290 and 270 million years ago – the primary clay, soft enough to be washed out by water, having been developed from felspar crystals in the hard granite: they are recognizable by their pearly sheen. They were altered in structure to minute platelets by superheated steam and gases welling up from the still-molten core of the Earth. With exposure to extremes of weather for inconceivable lengths of time, this Primary clay developed some plasticity – the flat platelets sliding over each other in a gel of silica; they can be seen through an electron microscope if you

17 Hand. Raku (Jill Crowley)

18 Mermaid, stoneware *(Jill Crowley, 1988)*

magnify them 30,000 times.

Potters know this refractory, pure white substance as kaolin or china clay. A major industry has developed from its extraction in Devon and Cornwall during the last 200 years, but Chinese potters have used a similar but more plastic clay for over 2000 years. The china clays found in Britain and the USA are too crumbly for making hollow forms by themselves, but if mixed with other plasticizing and fluxing materials it becomes the bony skeleton which holds its form when fired to a state of transluscent vitrification – porcelain – even up to 1500°C (2732°F). Kaolin, raw or calcined, is also an important glaze material.

The ball clays are much more plastic than china clay because the platelets were broken down to an even smaller particle size on their short tumultous journey to the lakes in the valleys. They remained remarkably pure, apart from additions of mineral potash and carbon from decayed vegetation, and so can be fired to their own vitrification point at temperatures of around 1300°C (2372°F). Though not transluscent, they are then watertight without glazing and are therefore defined as stoneware.

All clays have similar origins, some having been carried many miles before the current slowed down so that they could sink to the river or lake bottom; red and yellow clays picked up iron oxide colourants on the way, others became mixed with lime. Both these are fluxes that lower the practicable firing temperature to below 1100°C (2012°F), so that the clay is still porous and needs glazing to hold water; this is the definition of earthenware. If fired too high, they slump and eventually become a molten mass.

These transported clays are all referred to as Secondary, whilst fireclay is classified as Tertiary, having undergone yet another process – the fluxes being drawn out by the roots of growing plants and trees of the Carboniferous Age, which have since turned into coal. Consequently it is coarse-grained, refractory, and not very plastic. Mixed with other clays it can, however, be interesting to use, though only in thick sections as it does not have great structural strength before firing. Until the last 30 years all kilns were lined with fireclay brick (firebrick) backed with low-temperature insulation – now superseded by aerated kaolin mixtures which are both refractory and insulating.

Awareness of the rational sequence of geological events by which clays were formed helps us to understand their nature, as well as giving the feeling that we too are bringing about geological processes in miniature every time we fire our kilns – creating igneous rocks never seen before.

Our system of preparing clay is very simple, and the quantity is, after all, small compared to the needs of a throwing potter. Besides an ordinary small-bore potters' pug-mill, our only equipment consists of four open-topped wooden casks (18-gallon kilderkins), a long thin paddle for stirring, and eight strong boards of tongued and grooved wood held together by battens (about 80 × 30 cm [30 × 12 in]). It happens that we like to use equipment made of natural materials, preferably interesting in itself. We picked up our beechwood paddle on Brighton beach, part of a dismembered deck chair redolent of sunny picture-postcard days, but of course any non-rusting material could be used equally well.

The ball clay we now use is Hyplas 64 from a North Devon pit. We buy it in powder form, preferring this to nuts or shredded because any naturally-occurring iron pyrites have been drawn out by magnets, thus avoiding the development of catastrophic black craters during firing. The minimum order direct from Devon is 1000 kg (a ton), supplied in 25 kg ($\frac{1}{2}$ cwt) bags. This quantity will make a stack of about 0.16 cu. m. (6 cu. ft), but it can be obtained from Stoke-on-Trent in smaller quantities. It will store indefinitely as long as it is kept dry and the bags are not punctured. Mice find that both paper and polypropylene, well chewed, make very desirable nesting material, and even a tiny hole will let out a thin stream of powder clay that spreads rapidly. To improve the working texture and lessen shrinkage, we add 20 per cent of virgin fireclay grog, 32nds to dust – meaning new fireclay that has been prefired (not reclaimed firebrick), pulverized and passed through a sieve with a mesh size of a thirty-second of an inch.

The method is to pour about 27l (6 gal) of water into the cask, then gradually add two bags (i.e. 50 kg [110 lb]) of powdered clay, and 10 kg (22½ lb) of grog, stirring thoroughly. It is advisable to wear a simple dust-mask, available from any chemist, to make sure of avoiding silicosis. The four casks are used in rotation so that the clay can mature for as long as possible. During this process algae grow in the silica gel, increasing the sliding of the particles over each other. The wood of the casks becomes impregnated with beneficial micro-organisms that inoculate the next batch. Leaving some wet clay for continuity would fulfil the same purpose in a plastic bin.

To keep the clay clean, a cloth is draped over the top of the cask before the head is placed on top. By the time we have finished using one batch, most of the water will have evaporated from the next. The soft clay is then scooped out onto the boards, pushed up into high thin ridges for maximum surface exposure to drying air. It will be ready to feed into the pug-mill just before the thinnest edges are too hard, but if not wanted at once the moisture content will even out in a well-tied plastic bag.

If put through the pug-mill twice, this makes a good throwing body on its own. Pugged a second time with its own weight of T-material, and finished off by rotary kneading in both directions, it is superb for handbuilding. The final receipe is thus 40 per cent ball clay, 10 per cent fireclay grog, and

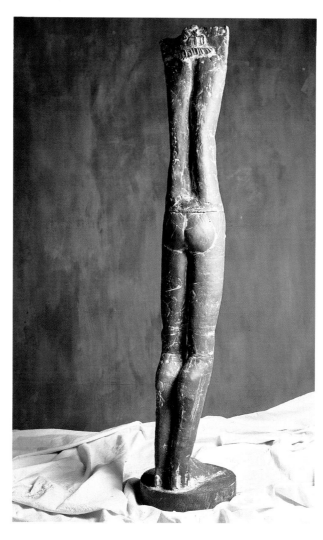

19 Standing Woman, height 2 m (6 ft) (Mo Jupp)

50 per cent T-material. Fired to 1260–1280°C (2300–2336°F), it becomes creamy white oxidized and light grey reduced; it has a linear shrinkage of one in ten. Hyplas 64 is not commercially available in plastic form, so there is no alternative to mixing this body yourself if you wish to make use of the quite exceptional green (i.e. unfired) strength of the clay found only in this particular pit. It may be that clays with similar qualities exist in other countries – suppliers will send you analyses and small quantities to try out.

It is remarkable how silky the clay will become as the weeks pass after pugging – even three or four days makes a difference to the workability. It is well worth trying to be sufficiently well organized to prepare the next batch a month ahead.

There would seem to be no need here to go into details about materials to cover the great range of possibilities for decoration; they are the same as for any other sort of pottery. Firing temperatures for clay, glazes, and decoration must, of course, be compatible. Controlled patterns are always a problem, and some of the solutions, other peoples' as well as our own, can be found in chapters 4 to 9.

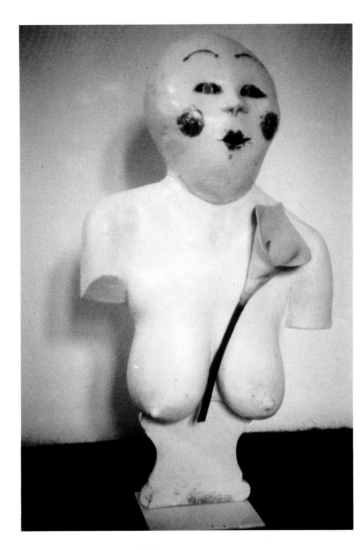

20 Doll (Mo Jupp)

3 EQUIPMENT AND ITS USES

Individuals vary greatly in their need for equipment. Some (mostly men) delight in making tools; others (mostly women) are happy to use whatever comes to hand. This is not improvization but a recognition that something unconventional will exactly fill a need – it most definitely does not mean putting up with an inadequate substitute. It can be difficult to explain to the well-meaning that one really does not want it replaced with a 'proper' bought tool.

My decorating tool is a good example. Used for incizing lines in soft clay, it started life as the spiked leg of a pair of compasses belonging to my grandfather – maybe broken off by one of his numerous children. Its chamfered brass handle is a pleasure to hold, and the spike keeps itself worn down to make exactly the right type of line. No bought tool could be better!

Austerity in equipment holds the same appeal as austerity of form. I like to think of our work as being a matter of ourselves, the clay, and the fire, but paraphernalia inevitably accumulates. The following fairly detailed description of our workshop and those things that play some essential part in making the job flow through smoothly is given not as a checklist but as a basis for variation. It may not apply at all to your way of working but will show the sort of points to take into consideration.

WORKSHOP

Having had many years of workshops that were spacious but out in the garden, with kilns yet another weather-dodging walk away, we now enjoy the luxury of a workshop under the house roof. For two people to work in reasonable harmony – with three dogs and a cat or two sharing the comforts – it is necessary to be well-organized. There are well-defined areas and shelves for work in different stages, samples and pieces actually for sale, a table for the telephone and paperwork. There are windows on both sides overlooking our garden, the lane and fields towards the village, steep wooded hills and the Wrey Brook; as the long axis is north-south the light is good, but direct sun not troublesome. A separate outside door provides direct access for potential customers and visitors.

The unexpectedly carpeted floor is kept conscientiously clean with a vacuum cleaner.

It might be thought that a large room was essential to contain all our needs, but in fact it is only 5.2 m by 3.4 m (17 ft by 11 ft). Its miniature scale amazes prolific throwing potters, but in it we manage very happily to earn our living. A couple of stables outside house the overflow – bulk clay, packaging, and the varied things that 'might come in handy'.

CLAY PREPARATION

For making up sizeable quantities of clay from powder form, casks or bins and a pug-mill are needed (as already described). For smaller quantities starting with plastic clay, a wire and scraper, with a good strong bench are entirely adequate. This should be just the right height so that you can straighten your back as you wedge, and lean on your straightened arm for spiral kneading. The bench top can be of wood or slate – clay will stick to a shiny surface. A butcher's block is admirable, or a length from a tree-trunk say

21 Blackbirds preening, stoneware (Terry Bell-Hughes)

60 cm (2 ft) in diameter, planed on the end grain.

WHEEL

For animals or figures based on thrown shapes, potters' wheels of any type can be used, but it is as well to set up with one able to take a greater weight of clay than you expect to be using. It is, as with kilns, always surprising how one's ambitions develop – potters thrive on challenges.

WORKING TABLE

This needs to be absolutely rigid and of comfortable height (rather lower than the wedging bench if you are going to work sitting down). Mine is 66 cm (26 in) high, as I am not tall; the work is brought up another 10 cm (4 in) by the turntable. The tabletop has room for propping up sketchbooks and other pieces for reference within reach but out of the way. Its surface too needs to be slightly absorbent, of wood planed but unpolished, dressed slate (a billiard table or fishmonger's slab), or good-quality plywood. Coils of clay can then be rolled out without sticking. Keep the top clean and smooth with a scraper, being careful to avoid scarring it with holes or dents, which would leave their mark on every piece of clay; tiny pieces of hard clay are likewise a menace, so keep them and the dust wiped away with a squeezed-out sponge or dishcloth.

CHAIRS

A chair that fits your physique can contribute enormously to your outlook on life, so take the trouble to choose one that is neither too high nor too low, not too deep nor too shallow. Backaches never helped anyone, and can be avoided by comfortable posture – perhaps with a cushion in the small of the back. Not everyone will be lucky enough to find, as I did, a very sculptural Arts and Crafts period chair amongst their aunt's effects! It has wide flat arms that support my elbows and is one of my most valuable tools. The separate decorating table is complemented by an old-fashioned swivel office chair of shaped wood that we found thrown out on a skip; my partner, who does our decorating, is taller than me, so his table, chair, and turntable are all higher.

TURNTABLE

A turntable is a necessity for three-dimensional thinking. It needs to be heavy for durability, and not too high, in order to avoid the tension caused by raising the shoulders. Mine is of cast iron, 20 cm (8 in) in diameter by 10 cm (4 in) high, weighing 4 kg (9 lb); objects of all sizes from tiny to 91 cm (3 ft) long have been constructed on it without difficulty. For very high pieces the turntable can stand on a stool lower than the tabletop.

WORKBOARDS

Smooth boards will be needed on which to work; they must be robust. Ours are of 2.5 cm (1 in)-thick wood. Any lengthwise joints should be glued, and the ends cleated to prevent warping. The one that gets used most is 28 cm × 23 cm (11 in × 9 in); others go up to 76 cm × 30 cm (30 in × 12 in). It is not comfortable to reach across greater widths.

LIGHTING

Proper lighting is essential. Strip lighting is useless because it flattens form. Daylight really needs to come from behind you, but makers of living creatures will probably want to look out at those that pass by, so the best compromise is to have the window on your left if you are right-handed. At night several light sources are necessary, otherwise the shadows will be too dark: one above and one behind the work, with an adjustable lamp to your left to bring out the forms, as well as low-level general lighting.

CLAYBINS

It is important to keep clay tidy and in perfect condition for the job in hand, with no hard crumbs lying around. My system is to have a cask beside the working table to take the clay direct from the pugmill; it needs to be kept damp by being sprayed inside occasionally. An enamel can with a plate on top takes several kneaded lumps for immediate use. A smaller lidded casserole is for all the offcuts, put in before they become too stiff; as the work goes on they are kneaded into the next lump, either to stiffen it or (splashed with water beforehand) to soften it. Small white-hard bits go in a little bowl for soaking down. Recycling is thus continuous, with no accumulation to deal with. Plastic containers are more usual for storage, we just find them lacking in interest.

SMALL TOOLS

All potters use a stranded wire with little wooden handles at either end for cutting clay, and keep a small natural sponge and jug of water to hand, as well as a thin fettling knife, maybe made out of a broken hacksaw blade. For our smooth coiling a firm kidney-shaped rubber and a wooden beater are needed, with the incising spike already mentioned (stuck safely into a cork when not in use). Other people's tools will be mentioned later, but pottery is not like woodwork in requiring a host of specialized tools for specific purposes. Most are adapted from other uses as need arises.

DECORATING TABLE

Materials and equipment for glazing need to be kept separate from clay, as even a tiny amount of cobalt oxide, for instance, distributed through a batch of clay could ruin many pieces of work with unwanted blue spots. Our decorating table holds many small pots of glaze, so it is long, with a vertical board at the back to prevent them slipping off. It, too, must be strong and rigid. The turntable is high enough to clear the glazes and brushes; the colours are carefully organized with the whites raised up on a small box to avoid contamination, and the cobalt in a corner of its own. There is a window immediately to the right and an Anglepoise lamp to supplement it; for our precise painting, the edges of the incised lines need to be sharply defined.

GLAZE-MAKING EQUIPMENT

This is kept on another bench with storage shelves or cupboards handy. It should be beside a sink with (preferably) hot as well as cold water. Besides scales, sieves of 80's mesh for slip, 120's for glazes, and 200's for oxides, there can never be too many vessels, since mixtures have to be sieved from one to another, or too many store jars. Brushes are needed for sieving, paddles and spoons for

stirring. Pestles and mortars may not be vital but save some of the sieving as well as being satisfying to use.

DRYING AND FIRING

Finished clay work must dry in a controlled way. As the water added to the clay evaporates, the solid particles move closer together, and the whole piece becomes noticeably smaller. If it dries more quickly in one part than another, it will first warp and then crack apart. Beginners soon find that two pieces of clay must be more or less equally moist or they will soon separate through differential shrinkage.

My work is covered with a plastic bag every time I leave it until it is complete. It is then moved around, drying in stages, finishing in a drying cupboard. We happened to find a large strong wooden packing case with a lid which, standing on its side, is ideal for our scale of work, taking the largest pieces that the kiln will hold. Two tubular greenhouse heaters stand on the bottom; these are designed to be safe in damp conditions, and are wired into a thermostat rod in the top set to 37.8°C (100°F). Above the heaters is a boot-scraper grid resting on bricks. Gaps have opened between the boards of the packing case, allowing the water-laden air to escape (a gently moving current is needed, not static hot air). We had many pieces spoilt by numerous fine cracks before we realized the importance of ample

22 Turkeycock, height 30 cm (12 in). Hollow form with added modelling and sprigged feathering, coloured with slips and touches of glaze. Reduction fired stoneware (Jeremy James, 1988)

ventilation – our previous drying cupboard had been too well made!

The pieces now stay around on the workboards at room temperature until they begin to go white-hard in patches; they then move onto flat slate roofing-tiles on the top of the drying cupboard (which they share with our mother cat, a jealously-guarded privilege). When white almost all over, they go inside the cupboard but raised well above the grid on a kiln shelf, still resting on their slates so that the bases dry out last. This is very important – the base, it seems, can absorb compression by the shrinking walls which it releases gently during its own shrinkage a rule that holds good for even very large pieces. If dried first, the bases invariably crack because they cannot pull the walls in with them. Finally, after a day or two, they go on their sides directly on the bars for one night at least. They are then tested for a few seconds, whilst still hot, on a cold slab of slate – when ready for the kiln, no damp patch will appear underneath. Since adopting this system we have had virtually no cracking.

If clay is not apparently dry before going into the kiln, the expansion of the water that inevitably still remains will cause cracks or, worse, blow up the piece to fragments. This caution continues during the firing itself: our biscuit programme raises the temperature by 50°C (122°F) per hour for the first two hours, then by 75°C (167°F) per hour for the next three. By 350°C (662°F) all physically-combined water will have been driven off, and as long as the clay is not in general more than 1.2 cm ($\frac{1}{2}$ in) thick the firing can be completed at 100°C (212°F) per hour. This should take it safely through the remaining hazards: driving off the chemically-combined water (the H_2O in the theoretical pure clay formula Al_2O_3 $2SiO_2$ $2H_2O$) at 550°C (1022°F), when the clay becomes pottery and cannot return to plasticity, and the next stage when the carbon is burnt out so that it does not cause bloating by becoming gaseous when sealed over in the higher glaze firing. It is sobering to think that 200 million years or so have passed since those two molecules of water were introduced at the time of the breaking down of the granite; and that the carbon consists of the decayed remains of trees and plants growing when the clay was washed down into the valleys around 50 million years ago.

We fire our biscuit to 900°C (1652°F) to retain porosity for glazing. The second, higher, firing to fuse the glazes begins much faster, slowing later to allow time for the irreversible chemical combination of the mixed ingredients. The temperature reaches 900°C (1652°F) in four hours, then rises at 75° (167°F) per hour to 1150°C (2102°F), slowing down to 45° (113°F) per hour up to the top temperature of 1260°(2300°F). We then soak it for one and a half hours, and finally cool slowly for two hours down to 900°C (1652°F). With our present small electric kiln the current is then switched off; seven hours later we open the lid a crack at 250°C (482°F), and eventually, after another three hours, the temperature has fallen to 150°C (302°F) and it is safe to unpack the kiln – having taken almost 24 hours from start to finish.

CHOOSING KILNS

Since firing temperature is the vital factor determining the characteristics of ceramics, it will be clear that the limitations are set by the available kilns. Given a choice, therefore, it is sensible to set up with a kiln that will do everything, i.e. firing to any temperature up to 1300°C (2372°F), with an oxidizing or reducing atmosphere at will. Your ideas can then change and develop without constraint.

Since the beginning of the Oxshott Pottery we have always had a gas kiln as a reliable standby, using it for earthenware (oxidized), stoneware (reduced), porcelain, and raku. In Surrey we used mains gas, in Devon we fire with bottled gas (propane). There have been coal kilns and coke kilns for stoneware and saltglaze, sawdust kilns, and a primitive 0.03 cu. m. (1 cu. ft) electric kiln. So far we have not experienced the delights – and hard work – of wood firing, with its incomparable results, nor felt ourselves sufficiently engineers to be drawn to use oil.

Our latest acquisition is a ceramic fibre/ LTM electric top-loader with digital pyrometer and microchip process control. It can be programmed to raise the temperature to any desired point up to 1300°C (2372°F) in three variable stages (ramps), as slowly or as fast as we choose; there can be a steady soaking period at the end of each ramp, and the rate of cooling can likewise be predetermined. A series of ten programmes can be fed into the memory and activated at will – at any time up to a week ahead – even operating an electric fan in appropriate conjunction.

This wonderful technical achievement is installed in the comfort of our workshop. Our clay matt glazes are better than ever before: they can now be soaked indefinitely at exactly top temperature – impossible to achieve manually. There is much more point in doing careful glaze tests as almost all the hazards of variation in speed and temperature have been removed. We hardly know we are firing! On the other hand, I personally miss the culminating excitement of pitting one's wits and skill against the wildcat element of fire; it would be a loss to start one's pottery experience with such a bland instrument. Also, any attempt to make a reducing atmosphere would remove the protective coating of oxide on the metal elements and considerably shorten their life – so oxidation must be accepted.

LIVING TOOLS

The only really vital tools are one's hands. People with disabilities can work wonders because they have a challenge to overcome; those of us with two hands in working order tend to take them for granted and are put out if they rebel – for instance at being suddenly asked to do too much. With even a slight understanding of their basic construction, we can do a great deal to keep these elaborate mechanisms well serviced so as to prevent future problems.

The bony joints are activated by muscles that shorten at will to make them move. Each bending muscle (flexor) is balanced by a stretching muscle (extensor). Continually pinching and gripping as we do, the flexors are developed and therefore pull down the extensors which, through lack of use, become weak, slack, and elongated. The system becomes unbalanced and we have aches and pains. The strain is passed on to the arms, which are set into the shoulders; we sit miserably hunched up with our aching hands, doggedly determined to finish our work, and soon the big trapezoidal muscle joining shoulders, neck, and the small of the back begins to complain – producing a headache and a stiff back . . .

Under these circumstances the work is unlikely to be much good! We would do better to take a break now and again for doing some stretching exercises to loosen up the whole bodily framework, working on each set of joints in turn. The vulnerable hand muscles can be helped in two ways: first by pulling the joints straight with the extensor muscles, so as to develop them too, and secondly by stretching the flexor muscles against the edge of the table or by pushing each finger back separately with the other hand. Another way is to link the fingers of your two hands together, turn them palm outwards and straighten your elbows, pushing away again and again. It hurts, but with perseverence there is a great feeling of well-being as the joints become able to make movements nearer their full potential and the muscles relax their tension. Clicks and creaks are a sign of successful manipulation!

One more point – clay is heavy stuff! If you are humping it around, remember the rule for avoiding a slipped disc: straighten your back, look up, and lift from the knees. The upper leg muscles are the strongest, so use them, not your vulnerable back.

This awareness of the articulation of the human body is also important as a starting point in relation to the construction of other creatures, with their different proportions and range of movements. For me, the transition from human to animal is through dancing and mime – inner feeling as much as external observation.

4 WORKING TO A THEME

We often look too far away to find a theme for our work; personal interests and innate gifts seem just the natural order of things, available to everyone and of no particular interest.

This is not, of course, true. Each person sees life differently, and art – amazingly – enables others to see through the eyes of the artist. There is no need to try to be different: it is inevitable. A potter's development comes best in small stages, with occasional leaps when the mine is worked out; otherwise one can all too easily become bogged down in a morass of unresolved problems.

To give an example, the eleven illustrations in Figs. 23, 25–31 and 33–35 cover my own 40-year exploration of a deliberately limited theme. They do not show major works which would more suitably belong elsewhere, but modest pieces that have stayed around because they are particularly meaningful to me.

To begin in 1950: with five years of art school and college training behind me, and having been brought up in my parents' pottery, I found myself a capable and sensitive thrower, thanks to Helen

Pincombe's teaching. I had a smattering of industrial techniques and was appreciative of a wide range of ceramics but without any sense of a path to follow. I had learnt that there had to be clay in my hands for creativity to flow, so design for mass-production was not for me; and I treasured an assurance from my sculpture teacher, Willi Soukop, that my strongest asset was a good sense of form – but I had no idea how to make use of it. He also said 'Be careful not to be funny', which I now understand to mean 'Beware of treating yourself, your work, and your subject as not worthy of being taken seriously'.

I was, of course, exceptionally lucky to be able to work at home. Floundering about with every encouragement to try out various possibilities – painted tin-glaze mugs, feathered slipware flower-pots – it was surprising and very reassuring to find that the London shops to whom we regularly sold the work of our pottery were most encouraging and seemed prepared to buy whatever I made. It must be said that there were few established studio potteries and little competition!

At this time some potters, following an ethic imported from Japan, felt that clay should be used only to make wares of simple beauty and exclusively utilitarian nature, preferably wheel-thrown in series. Others were feeling that a vessel could justifiably be seen as an individual work of art. A very few were inspired by the recent (1948) London art gallery exhibition of astonishing work by Picasso, who pointed out a route by which artist-potters could escape from the usual confines of the vessel. By cutting and joining thrown forms he had turned them, with a few of his inimitable brush-strokes, into animals, birds, or people by alluding rather than describing. These were immensely exciting but the technique I found somewhat immobile (*Fig. 24*).

Nor could I settle down to repetition throwing, finding it boring. It was all very difficult! Two solutions temporarily arose: individual pots for flowers, and clay people made by adding to a simple thrown bottle shape. These were made respectably 'useful' by endlessly carrying dishes or electric lights on their uncomplaining heads, or by becoming containers for oil or

vinegar (*Fig. 23*). There were many historical antecedents, but mine were based on the sensitively-modelled eighteenth- to

23 Thrown Ladies, height 21 cm (8¾ in). Right: saltglaze (1951). Left: incised glaze over iron wash (RDW)

24 Picasso's Horseman, thrown and assembled (Victoria and Albert Museum)

nineteenth-century saltglaze of La Borne near Bourges in central France.

Very occasionally in one's lifetime events conspire to provide just what is needed at the right time. Such was the appearance of Francine Delpierre and Albert Diato, potters from France who were catapulted into my life, taught me just what I needed, and disappeared. With their flanged and shaped strip technique for constructing not only pots but animals and birds based on a Mediterranean tradition, and an injunction to simplify – 'If in doubt, suppress!' – I was free to put together my abilities and my interests. Fig. 23 also shows the last of the thrown ladies, not 'useful' but much more alive: it is, in fact, a portrait of Francine.

The sheep in Fig. 25 is an early example of my use of their method, made in 1956 out of clay from a bank in a remote Lake District farmstead, loud with bleating. This was in the museum study stage; it followed an Assyrian carving in hard stone. Beginning, as shown in chapter 5, with a pinched pot, four balls were welded on for the feet. The edge was then cut flat with scissors or a fettling knife, the walls being a series of flanged strips; the flanges are worked down progressively with the thumb, first one side then the other, with a final pinching all round. The corners at the shoulders and haunches were preformed before joining, and so on until the hollow form was eventually closed with a small plug. Being full of air, it could then be beaten and worked over with a

25 Ullswater Sheep, length 14 cm (5½ in) made from coils flattened, flanged and shaped. Local clay (RDW, 1956)

kidney-shaped rubber tool. Finally, to let the steam out during firing, holes were cut for the eyes – and miraculously the clay came to life and looked back at the maker! The fleece was suggested by a spiral pattern, sandpapering some areas and burnishing others. It was really surprising to find that I could make the clay creature appear to be alive in the same way as my puppets and marionettes, although they cannot actually move.

The circus horse in Fig. 26 belongs to this period of rectangular stylization, though it was in fact made later. I had been watching Laurence Olivier's film of Shakespeare's *Henry V* and my mind was filled with heraldic pageantry. Cutting holes to lighten the mane and tail emphasized the hollowness; for the same reason the saddle is a lid.

26 *Circus Horse, length 20 cm (8 in) with acrobatic clowns on saddle-shaped lid (RDW)*

Compared to throwing, the hand-building technique was very slow, and it seemed impossible that I could charge high enough prices to make more than an occasional piece practicable. I tried slip-casting from the original hand-built pieces, but what was the point of spending my time in making copies in clay untouched by human hand? The resulting orders for making these cheaper pieces in quantity were intimidating. Open-top American Indian bird pots (*Fig. 9*) suggested an interesting formalization, so occasional hand-built creatures to hold flowers joined the thrown pots – few of which remained straightforwardly circular by then. This was the mixture for my first London exhibition, at Heal's, a department store well known for its appreciation of the crafts (1957).

Fate again stepped in. A serious operation left me without strength to throw for some months, though with intensive practice, hand building became less slow. Concentration on its possibilities brought dissatisfaction with the 'ethical demand' for utility as the only worthwhile form of use. This limited view now appeared as mere self-justification on the part of the buying public for the very British inability to make conscious aesthetic choices. Surely a flower arrangement is only 'useful' because it is itself a work of art? Quite suddenly it became clear that my creatures must stand on their own feet, and likewise that I must learn to develop ideas from sources less second-hand.

27 Alderney bull forms, height 11 cm (4¾ in). Clay from bank on seashore with local granite dust, seaweed ash glaze (RDW, 1958)

28 Owl, height 36 cm (14 in), slightly saltglazed (RDW, 1967)

In a particular state of awareness, one can open one's mind and that which is sought comes of its own accord. With the consciousness of necessity I walked round with my eyes open – and two hens in their nest-box simplified themselves into clay shapes. Next came a potters' holiday on the island of Alderney, using clay from the cliff and mock-serious primitive firings of dried seaweed and driftwood. An Alderney bull tethered on a promontary contentedly chewing the cud became correlated with the sea-worn rocks (*Fig. 27*). Form for its own sake took over: the upright plane of the bull's back must curl round as far as possible before doubling back on itself like a wave – a shape-theme that I still use though with less austerity. Concavity was to be avoided: Willi Soukop had taught that living forms are invariably convex.

A more prestigious London exhibition followed, shared with my mother, Denise K. Wren, at the Berkeley Galleries in Davies Street (1960). Both of us showed pots as pots and creatures as creatures, all salt-glazed. Serious collectors appeared.

The bird-table drawings described in chapter 1 were a logical continuation after the hens and the bull. At last I was looking out on the natural world without fear of realism. The pigeons in Fig. 15 have legs that are the foot-ring of a pot, the seaweed-ash stoneware glaze being intended to grow naturally on the form like lichen.

Owl – now the presiding genius of a

29, 30 Cock and Hen. Raku with vanadium/selenium glaze on combs, copper alkaline glaze on neck, tail and wing feathers. Grogged ball clay (RDW, 1969)

patron's hearth – shows the hieratic quality imparted by the simplicity and starkness of these shapes (*Fig. 28*). The carefully-controlled use of coarse-grained carborundum paper on dry clay enabled planes to be clarified, the angles where they joined sharpened. This was a very productive period and I made animals that were as large as I could carry.

Potters of our sort thrive on challenges. It probably wasn't the dust (I could and should have worn a dust-mask) nor the way people said approvingly 'It looks just like wood!' (when it would be better looking like clay) but just the fact that I had carried it as far as I could that caused the rebellion. A raku party after a serious seminar in 1968 offered liberation from the careful planes and the anxieties of high firing in a solid-fuel kiln. Problems had arisen anyway as the right sort of coke was no longer being produced now that Britain had changed from coal-gas to natural gas from the North Sea; gas-fired kilns too needed new, experimental burners.

The immediacy of raku in the American manner demanded rapid, visible construction with coarsely-grogged clay. There could be lattice-work to acknowledge the hollowness (*Fig. 30*). Wickedly bright reds – forbidden territory to stoneware potters – were resplendent against the black background that resulted from plunging the red-hot pieces in sawdust; metallic lustres (unfortunately fugitive) appeared spontaneously in the soft copper glaze. Some

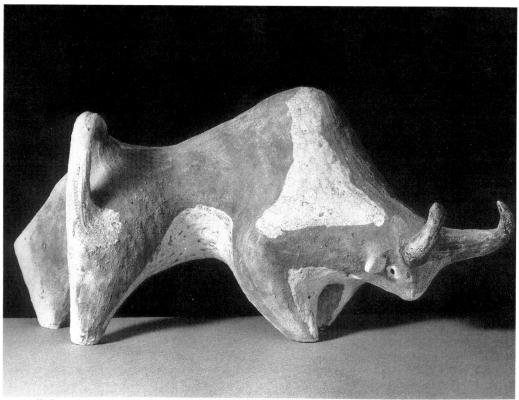

31 Bull, length 53 cm (21 in). Raku, grogged ball clay with white alkaline glaze (RDW, 1973)

valued collectors of my work were shocked, but most responded bravely.

The raku bull in Fig. 31 was made in the demanding circumstances of the circus ring at a potters' camp in 1971. With a hundred and more pairs of knowledgeable eyes

watching, it had to go right – no second thoughts!

The next two pieces are a branch line. I had been asked to make a hanging bird-table, perhaps a central cylinder with one dish attached below and another inverted above

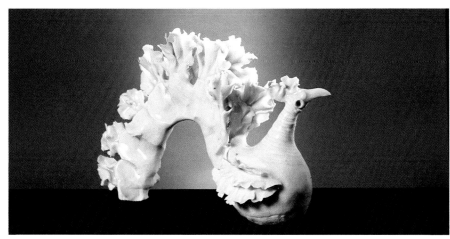

32 Chintz bird, length 20 cm (8 in). Porcelain, reduction fired to 1280°C (RDW, 1973)

33 Wrens – life-size series made between 1960 and 1989 (RDW)

as a roof. Translated into handbuilding this shape acquired a quite unexpected significance (*Fig. 34*). The central tubular feature became the core of an apple, visualized symbolically as Adam and Eve embracing; they are not readily discernible, being merely two curved pieces of raggedly pinched-out clay. Growing outwards from their hands and feet is the apple's skin, a shell enclosing the haven of their togetherness; from windows in this safe environment they look out at the world.

Fig. 35 is a further development of the same idea, entitled *Generations*. I found that the tubes, seen as architectural pillars, could be joined by arched vaulting, providing a platform through which holes could be pushed, their edges then able to be built up to form another storey – and so on, *ad infinitum* . . . . The tubular representatives of succeeding generations have roughly-suggested arms; they grow inseparably related to each other by their construction, and the process continues without defined completion.

This formation has many fascinations: it is totally three-dimensional, not easily amenable to making by anything other than hand-built clay, meaningless if drawn as plan and elevation; and if you follow the surface vertically the inside becomes the outside in a way that makes your head spin, the solids and voids flowing into each other alarmingly.

Only two of these ever found purchasers, and even so both of them felt compelled to

34 Adam and Eve inside the Apple of Life, diameter 20 cm (8 in). Grogged ball clay, biscuitted then sawdust fired (RDW, 1972)

35 Generations, diameter 30 cm (12 in). Biscuitted then sawdust fired (RDW, 1973)

put the holes to 'use' – one by filling them with pots of geraniums, the other with mineralogical specimens. Would this have happened if they had been cast in bronze and they had paid ten times the price? I couldn't, it seemed, carry my pottery-collecting public that far, though my own opinion is that they were probably nearer true sculpture than anything else I have ever made.

After this the porcelain birds (*Fig. 32*) were purely frivolous. My attempts to use this amazing clay body in a way that shows the beauty of its ability to hold its shape right up to transluscency were not happy. In the plastic state it easily stretched and flopped; it refused to do what I wanted, and would not make recognizable birds – Indian chintz birds with frilly tails were its limit. There is, I see, a new porcelain body on the market which may well be better (see Suppliers, p. 95).

To conclude this survey, Fig. 33 shows a series of wrens made between 1960 and the present day (1989); I have always enjoyed making my name-bird. After the problems of porcelain I returned with relief to stoneware – but this time finger-finished, not sandpapered. This takes the theme to the next chapter; beyond that, only time will show.

5 HOLLOW HANDBUILDING

Sculptural ceramics, based on the use of thin-walled forms, can be fairly flat or three-dimensional and hollow. They can be constructed carefully into a thought-out shape from the start, with round or flattened coils, with torn, pinched, or pressed-out pieces of clay, or by using moulds and patterns. Alternatively, a simple basic extruded tube, rolled sheet, or wheel-thrown pot can be altered by pushing from inside, adding from outside, or cutting apart and re-assembling when either quite firm or (more exciting) quite soft. Most clays will bond permanently if pressed firmly together whilst plastic, but when leather-hard can only be joined by being dampened, or smeared with very wet clay (slip or slurry). An understanding of the methods used seems to me essential for developing insight and informed appreciation, as it explains the great variety of possible results – as can be seen in chapters 7, 8, and 9.

There are two reasons for the thin walls: firstly, drying and firing are much more straightforward and, secondly, they make for greater sensitivity of form. They are more malleable, and deliberate distortion is easier:

a dull shape can be brought to life by a gentle nudge.

Roger Fry said of Chinese art: 'A painting was always conceived as the visible record of a rhythmic gesture. It was the graph of a dance executed by the hand'. To me, throwing and handbuilding at their best are likewise the visible record of a dance taking place in the mind. A satisfactory stressed-skin structure can result from a dressmaking technique – a dart cut out here, a gusset added there – but the natural flow as clay is added to clay defies imitation. It is important to recognize and trust the rare occasions when everything comes together, the clay is just right and 'genius is burning'. This state comes only as a reward for the hard labour of developing perception and dexterity. Fostering the ability to stand by and watch your hands working as the life-force flows through them is the true task of the artist; to set aside these demands leads only to frustration and disillusion.

My own technique of handbuilding is best shown by the diagrams in Fig. 36, which relate to the photographs of our current work, chosen to show possible solutions to

various constructional problems. Once the problem is isolated, the way out becomes apparent. All these have started with a drawing from life, clay then being used to make what I have drawn – not what my intellect tells me *ought* to be there. In this way one is using potent shapes that have struck the intuitive vision. It is vital to hold on to them, for intellectual alterations are fatal to the original conception. A certain amount of infilling can be incorporated as long as it is interpreted in the same broad way. A bird, for instance, might have been too far away for the details of its pattern to be clearly visible, but they can easily be found in a reference book.

It is important to keep the degree of stylization consistent; both naturalistic elements and additions produced mechanically (e.g. hair made of clay pushed through perforated zinc) will look out of place on a finger-finished or simplified creature.

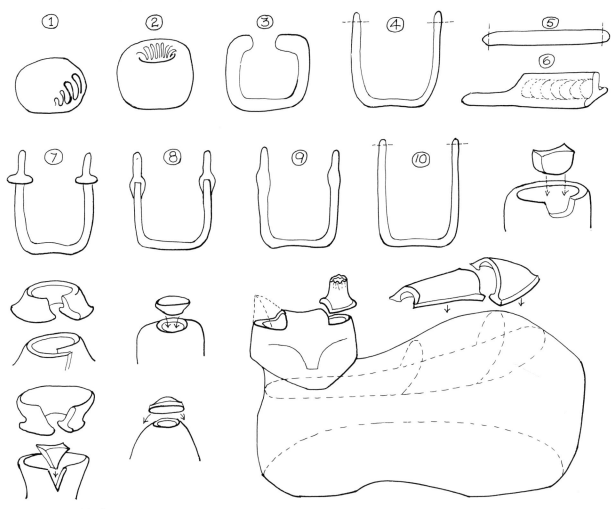

36 *Method of hollow construction using coils flattened, flanged and shaped*

SCULPTURAL FORM

The quality of sculpture comes from the way in which the forms are fitted together: working out what will happen where they join is the challenge and the fascination. The degree of success of the work as a whole depends almost entirely on the thoroughness with which these problems have been resolved. Watch the profile as the work rotates on the turntable, remembering that the voids are as important as the solids. With *Tim Cat*, for instance, the empty shape bounded by his back, tail, and head is as important as the body. Likewise when constructing the legs, their profile must also be seen as making the shape of the spaces they define. Pairs or groups give further scope for manipulating space, but to relate well they must be made at the same time – as were the long-tailed tits in Fig. 14.

Beaks are easy to fit onto birds' heads, but each variety has its own characteristics: compare the bluetits in Fig. 2 with the seagulls, (*Fig. 38*), the woodcock (*Fig. 39*), and the partridge (*Fig. 40*). A line has been used to emphasize the junction. It is much more difficult to make the transition from the shoulders to the head: compare the bluetits, the partridge, and the pigeons (*Fig. 41*) which have still smaller heads and longer, thinner necks with a wider range of movements. The drawing (*Fig. 42*) of the heron shows how its remarkable and unique neck was constructed in clay to give the

37 Tim Cat and the Calico Kitten, height 40 cm (16 in) and 23 cm (9 in). Both made from coils flattened, flanged and shaped. Stoneware (RDW/PMC, 1987)

38 Pair of seagulls, length 25 cm (10 in). White and yellow matt glazes with black cobalt oxide (RDW/PMC, 1987)

feeling of sinewy strength.

It is enlightening to set oneself exercises in pure three-dimensional geometry. For instance, start with a base that is triangular in plan, and on this build up walls that twist to arrive at a horizontal section with the triangle turned half round; continuing further up, the triangle has turned again to coincide with the plan of the base. The variations are infinite and can be gradated in a subtle way like Bach fugues.

If you are working from a drawing,

proportion is often surprising. Having made the base, the piece must be a certain height to give the same proportions, but measuring the drawing and increasing in scale does not inevitably produce the expected result. Volume comes into it, and the eye is the only judge. Maquettes – small, quickly-made models – are sometimes helpful but will often need adaptation for structural reasons.

Feel the bone structure under the clay although it is only in your mind. A bird's wing may be simplified to surface pattern or

even just a line, but can nevertheless hold the strength that can fly many hundreds of miles, to the Arctic, to Africa. It is helpful to have some idea at least of how our skeletons relate to those of other creatures; badgers, for instance, place the whole of their back feet on the ground as we do, whereas dogs and horses stand on their toes: their hocks are our heels. This kind of information will save you from making joints bend the wrong way, frequently seen in ill-observed renderings of elephants and amphibians.

Long furry coats (Tim Cat, *Fig. 37*), sheep's wool (*Fig. 43*), and fluffed-out feathers are a different problem – that of putting clay round a form that is mostly air, so that it actually looks light and airy. Angles are always important at points where the form changes direction, for definition, variety, and strength. Edges, too, need great care: decide exactly where, and how, the inside is to meet the outside. There are ways of giving an impression of thinness and delicacy beyond that allowed by the clay – for instance by keeping one surface flat and bringing the other over the top to meet it on one side of the edge. A professional result comes from making a whole series of minute decisions.

39 Woodcock, length 33 cm (13 in). Shiny high-iron glaze contrasted with matt of various colours (RDW/PMC, 1987)

40 *Partridge, height 18 cm (7 in). Hollow, decoration incised and brush-painted. Reduction fired stoneware (RDW/PMC, 1986)*

41 Pair of Fantail Pigeons, length 23 cm (9 in), as taken from biscuit firing (RDW, 1988)

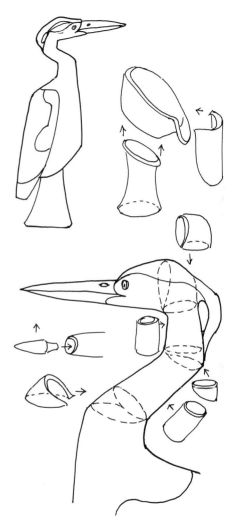

42 Heron – showing construction

MOVEMENT AND EXPRESSION

A turning shape has movement following right through, even though the creature is still. Watching our Calico Kitten (*Fig. 37*) standing on tiptoe, one could sense a line of tension from her toes to the tip of her tail, taut as the male partner in Spanish flamenco dancing, his castanets rhythmically building up the intensity. I have never cared for horses that gallop forever off the end of the mantelpiece, my preference being for creatures that are quiet and watchful, for moments of poise, of stillness between movements; they are more peaceful to live with, like Chinese inward-turning compositions.

Expression is given by the sum total of the whole attitude – it is not something added to the face when the rest is finished. One tends not to look at the work as a whole, so it is important to get up and look at it from across the room, and to make use of the way your own work takes you by surprise when you return, having been out. It is amazing how difficult it is to see what one has actually made, as distinct from the picture in one's mind. If a detail will not fit properly it is either because it is not, in fact, necessary, being encompassed already, or (worse) because the form of which it should be the logical outcome is in some way wrong. This can mean drastic alteration which it is most unpleasant to have to admit! The solution is usually to start again and build on your experience.

There comes a point when everything is there but somehow does not make a whole. It needs pulling together; so pick up your kidney rubber, take your courage in both hands and work with broad, sweeping gestures just making shapes – forget the meaning and the laboured detail. The transformation can be magical!

DECORATION

The heraldry of plumage and fur serve a definite purpose: their patterns, organized into absolute clarity, are there for recognition by friend or foe. They retain their basic arrangement but change in proportion as the creature moves. We, however, have a static clay object to put them on, and so take typical elements of the living pattern and adapt them to suit our own shapes. The pattern of the woodcock, for instance, is drastically simplified (*Fig. 39*). The intention is that the pattern should fit right round the

43 Jacob's sheep with lamb, length 21 cm (8½ in). Stoneware (RDW, 1986)

44 Tortoiseshell Cat with her kitten. Contrasting matt and shiny glazes (RDW/PMC, 1987)

clay with a look of inevitability, defining the form. Often the pattern can allude (as on the Cycladic and the Picasso horsemen, Figs. 3 and 24) to legs or other features that were not three-dimensionally convenient. Using my spike tool on cheese-hard clay I draw and re-draw until the shapes on both sides of the lines are full and rich; this developing process can continue for as long as the clay is sufficiently moist to smooth over completely.

The clay creature, likewise, can have colour that is expressive of the qualities of ceramics. Keeping in a general way to the tone patterns of nature – the play of light and dark – it is interesting to contrast matt and shiny glazes, as on the tortoiseshell mother cat with her kitten (*Fig. 44*), and the woodcock (*Fig. 39*). Thin washes of oxide (we use pure cobalt for black) can be set against thick clay matt glazes or vitrified slip; this is shown effectively in the seagulls (*Fig. 38*).

Our glazes are painted onto the biscuit with a brush – a process that sounds deceptively easy. In fact it takes even longer than the making stages; unless carried out with meticulous care, it just looks messy. The fantail pigeons in Fig. 41 are shown just as they come out of the biscuit kiln. The burrs pushed up by the incising tool are best rubbed off at this stage with carborundum (a scythe hone broken into convenient sizes). Small Chinese brushes are ideal for painting because the hairs are long enough to hold the glaze well and have just the right amount of spring. The piece is held so that the light emphasizes the edge of the line, and the thickness suitable to the particular glaze is built up stroke by stroke, as can be clearly seen in the partridge (*Fig. 40*).

Wet glaze on top of dry will cause blistering, which must be rubbed over with the finger tips or the palm of the hand. Lifted areas of matt glazes will not sink back in the kiln but fire as thin semi-detached fragile shells above the clay surface. Care must be taken in handling to avoid transferring unwanted colour from one 'compartment' to another, or rubbing thin patches in a finished surface. Work out a logical order of decoration; keep your hands scrupulously grease- and glaze-free. We finish our work in one firing by using glazes which mature together. Certain imperfections can be touched up and refired. As a technique this is very tedious, but the results can be rich and varied.

6 MOULDS

The ceramics industry reproduces identical pieces in quantity by the use of porous moulds made of plaster of Paris. The replicas must be released cleanly, so their shapes are necessarily limited. Ways of using moulds more freely will be mentioned in the following chapters. My own student piece *The Goat Girl* – a romanticized self-portrait based on eighteenth-century mantelpiece ornaments – will serve to give a condensed illustration of the process. There are books and short courses from which the details can be learnt; alternatively you can take your original model to one of the professional mould-makers who advertise in the ceramic press.

The Goat Girl group was first completed, the shapes being solid as there was no intention of putting it through the kiln. It was then carefully shorn of detail using a fine wire, and cut into six sections, each demanding a separate mould; some of them were in two pieces, others in more – a total of 17 pieces in all. The tree, being flat, was best made as a press mould using plastic clay; the remainder could be cast in slip. For this purpose a thick clay slurry of a suitable body mixture is thinned down into fluid slip by the addition of a very small quantity of sodium silicate and soda ash (suppliers' catalogues will give recipes). This manipulation of the acid-alkali balance minimizes the water content, thereby greatly reducing shrinkage and consequent distortion.

After the casting was completed and the main shapes were fettled and assembled, the leaves were made as separate sprigs in small, shallow press-moulds and applied to the tree. The individual hand-modelled touches were limited to the girl's hat, the horns and ears of the goats, the bird in its nest, and the fruit, flowers, and vegetation. As a student in a college that was going through an industrial design phase, one was expected to be satisfied with this cost-effective means of production; and indeed it could have been financially lucrative, for master moulds, once made, can be copied again and again in plaster to avoid any further time-consuming original work. However, I found it all very tedious and Fig. 45 shows the whole extent of a very limited edition! The clay body was a vitrified earthenware; the decoration encompassed underglaze, onglaze enamels, and lustre, involving three or four firings.

If you want to teach yourself something of the various ways of making and using moulds, sprigs are straightforward as a beginning. They can be seen as medallions on the Peruvian bull (*Fig. 12*) and as the leaves on the goat girl's tree. Think the whole job right through and collect everything necessary before you start: once mixed, plaster sets with alarming rapidity. Keep the whole process well away from good clay as even a tiny piece of plaster, embedded in the clay, can lie dormant during firing but eventually swell and push a large flake off the finished piece. Cover the tabletop with plenty of newspaper to facilitate clearing up the inevitable mess.

You will need dental-quality plaster of Paris from a chemist or potters' supplier, a wide-mouthed jug, a tablespoon, a large bowl or bucket, and access to water. Sprigs are best carved in reverse on a smooth flat block of plaster, so, taking a piece of plate glass larger than the intended block, set up a containing wall on its surface. The wall can be of clay, of linoleum tied with string to

45 Goat Girl, height 19 cm (7½ in). Slip-cast, press-moulded and sprigged. Vitrified earthenware (RDW, 1949)

water in the jug, judging the volume to be rather less than the eventual block (this ability comes with practice). Make sure the tablespoon is dry, open the bag of plaster and quickly but carefully shake it in spoonfuls over the whole surface of the water. There is enough when it begins to appear above the surface; then stir right down to the bottom, gently to avoid trapping air. If the mixture is just right and the plaster of good quality, it will start to set in a few minutes. Pour it slowly into the containing wall so that the angles are properly filled, jog the glass a few times to settle the top, and immediately turn your attention to washing the jug and spoon in the bowl of water. The plaster that washes off will sink to the bottom of the bowl and begin to set there as well; this is the reason for using a bowl rather than letting the washings go down a drain (unless it is fitted with a proper settling trap). Reasonably clear-looking washing water can, however, be poured down a drain, the half-set plaster being wiped out with newspaper or dug out with a metal tool if necessary. A flexible polythene bowl can be bent to dislodge really hard plaster.

As soon as the plaster block is firm, you can strip off the walls and tidy the corners or any unevenness (ideally with a mould-maker's palette of flexible metal). It will be half an hour or so before the block is strong enough to slide off the glass, with the help of water as a lubricant. After leaving it to dry in a warm place overnight, carve out your

make a circle, or of four lengths of wood overlapped to make a rectangle. Allow plenty of extra height, seal the junctions thoroughly with clay, and provide buttresses against the thrust of the plaster.

Make sufficient plaster in one mixing. Put

sprigs, judging progress by pressing in a small ball of clay. The finished sprigs can be removed whilst still plastic by suction with a flexible blade after the back has been scraped flat, ready for attachment to the main shape with slight moisture or a smear of smooth slip.

Unmixed plaster easily absorbs moisture and loses its ability to set, so store it in an air-tight container and mix a teaspoonful or two as a test before starting a job. Turn it out in a little heap onto newspaper; after half an hour it should snap sharply in two.

Moulds for shapes that are not undercut can be cast in the same way, first sticking the model firmly to the glass with water or slip. Hollow replicas can then be made by simply pressing a layer of plastic clay over the inner surface and tidying the edges. The plaster will absorb water out of the clay, making it shrink so that the cast replica easily falls out. References to basic shapes made in this way will be found in the following three chapters.

The principle of casting in slip is much the same, but there will be greater shrinkage. Fill the mould to the top; soon a firm shell will develop, following the contours and detail exactly. When this looks sufficiently thick, pour out the fluid slip inside it for re-use.

The top edge of a slip-cast replica will, however, be thin unless you keep re-filling the mould as the level of the slip sinks. This can be avoided by casting a 'spare' on top to give extra depth; it is trimmed off during fettling. To make this, first fill the mould solidly with clay (unless the original model is still in place). On top of this stick a cylinder of clay about the size of your thumb; it must slope inwards towards the top. This will produce a hole which is the unavoidable sign of slip-casting. Cut several small hemispherical depressions (natches) in the plaster, which will fill to make corresponding 'noggles', keeping adjacent pieces aligned.

The exposed top surface of the plaster must now be treated with a releasing agent: a wash of clay slip, a good smearing of petroleum jelly, or (more professionally) several coats of specially-formulated soft soap. Then set up containing walls again, tied tightly against the sides of the first piece but projecting above them; pour in plaster as before, but leaving the top of the 'spare' uncovered. Dig this out when the plaster has set thoroughly, then run water into the hole and gently pull the two pieces apart. Sponge the mould clean and dry it out thoroughly before use. It will also need re-drying after several replicas have been made.

The moulds for many shapes will need to be made in a larger number of pieces so that they can be pulled away from the clay replica without catching on undercuts. The position of the seams must be decided by careful assessment before you start – excellent training for the eye in seeing exactly what shape you have actually made!

Separation of the pieces is achieved by partly burying the model, protected by tissue paper, in a series of clay nests that have horizontal top surfaces neatly fitted against the modelling at the seam-lines; make vertical walls as usual. As each piece is cast, leave it in place against the model so that the whole thing can be turned round sufficiently to cast the next piece up against it, re-settled in a new nest and walls. Professionals take pride in achieving a final rectangular block or cylinder that can be tied with string. Alternatively, an enclosing case can be cast with a thumb-hole for pushing out the piece-mould. Remember to include the 'spare', to cut natches, and to apply the releasing agent.

For press-moulding, the moulds are made in the same way but the filling hole must be larger to admit a ramming tool. Sometimes it is necessary to press clay into separate pieces of the mould, allowing it to stand proud of the edges; then apply a smear of slip and force the pieces together. The join will be much neater if a groove is cut to accommodate the surplus, just outside the seam-line.

Huge quantities of frost-proof architectural terracottas were produced in the nineteenth century by press-moulding. Gigantic pieces can be made in sections and joined after firing; there is scope here for far more ambitious work by makers of sculptural ceramics than is usual today, though a few are breaking the mental bonds of the pot-sized piece. Reproduction by means of press-moulds is by no means new, though before plaster was used they were made of porous biscuit (*see Fig. 16*).

7 THE HUMAN FIGURE – OTHER APPROACHES

This chapter and the two that follow are composed of contributions from twelve other makers of sculptural ceramics, chosen for their diversity of approach and technique. With two exceptions their photographs and explanations refer to present production – they have all used clay in other ways and will no doubt do so again. To give coherence, I decided to restrict the range to people who have workshops in Britain. Many more could have been included even without going overseas, so it is evident that after a period of abstract exploration of the material, interest has swung towards the figurative. To maintain an element of organization, the headings of the three chapters are given as Humans, Birds and Animals – an arbitrary division referring only to the ceramic examples illustrated.

The series opens with Stanislas Reychan, an emigré from Poland who worked in London for 30 years. Although he writes '. . . I fully realise that this "NOT – YET – Obituary" is far to long for your purpose' he continues '. . . but took this opportunity to mention things which I did not write about on a different occasion'. Such a graphic account of struggle and determination to win through, however, fulfils a historical purpose in this book. It is included verbatim as a tribute to the courage and zest for life of a maker of sculptural ceramics who, although unable now to see what he has typed, can write with wit and humanity as he embarks on his 92nd year (letter dated 3.1.1989).

STANISLAS REYCHAN

Gemini (Fig. 46); Bacchus (Fig. 47); Crocodile (drawing by RDW, Fig. 48)

SOURCES

I used a lot the Zodiac and the Twins are Gemini. I have not the slightest idea why I chose boys and not girls. They are certainly not 'portraits'. As far as I can remember I have made only two portraits – all of my many hundreds of figures are illustrations, interpretations or figments of imagination. The two are *Picture Hanging* and *The Old Priest*. I knew the two girls who helped to hang pictures at the Hampstead Show, and I saw the very old priest walking along the street every morning when having breakfast at my hotel at the Venetian Lido.

I almost always made two – and sometimes three or even more – identical figures at the same time. There have been two of *Picture Hanging* and two of your *Gemini* – I don't know who has bought the other. The colours may have been different but the design would be identical, owing to my working methods, without the use of moulds. *The Old Priest* was a success and was repeated five or six times.

TECHNIQUE

During my over 30 working years I never knew anyone using that way of modelling nor do I know how I started it. On several occasions I would show it and teach but it seemed not to be followed. Except throwing I used all other ways of pottery and modelling for other work, but all figures were made the same way which could be easier explained by drawing which I cannot do any more.

With my heavy African hardwood roller 40 inches long [1 m] and 5 diameter [125 mm] I roll the clay on a piece of cloth to about 2 or 3 mm thickness [$\frac{1}{8}$ in], cut out certain shapes, usually with a paper pattern, give them the necessary shape, sticking them together with slip and 'assembling' to a wanted figure. The *Gemini* consist of four oblong pieces, four oval larger and four small round ones. The first four (rolled) are the legs and the oval ones given an eggshell shape are the bodies and the smaller ones are the heads. It is like assembling a motorcar

and not 'artistic' at all. All my work in figures done in my studio was built in that way – large and small.

I never drew my figures in advance, I just 'saw' them in my head, cut out the relevant pieces of clay and got on with the 'assembly'. Vivid imagination? There were drawn lines for the paper patterns to be cut out in case of a repeat. The oval clay pancakes were pressed into a hollow plastercast to give it the shape of – say a quarter of the body of a rhino or half of the boy's body. The crocodile was entirely made in the air by hand. An 18-inch [45 cm] long pancake about 6 inches [15 cm] wide in the middle was dried for a short time on a round stick and then carefully held in the left hand whilst the sides were joined with slip and the basic body was ready.

But did not all the tiles, Xmas cards and medallions not need some drawing? Yes – a sort of drawing – an outline on the clay. The parts were cut out, applied on a tile as low relief and cast in plaster.

I designed certain small figures which

46 Gemini, height 28 cm (11 in). Rolled clay tubes, some press-moulding with added modelling, oxides painted on tin glaze. Earthenware (Stanislas Reychan)

seemed suitable for 'mass-production' whilst I was still at the Central [School of Art in London]: *Owlets* in two sizes and a pair of *Lion and Unicorn*. The owls were totally assembled but the pair needed a plaster cast for the base and the bottom part of the body. The rest – heads, legs and tails – had to be modelled on. I thought all of them suitable only for a white soft majolica glaze. At the time two diploma students – Lord Queensberry and Gordon Baldwin – made up a crazy recipe (now regarded as deadly poisonous) which nevertheless I mixed up and used almost exclusively for 30 years. When Eileen Lewenstein said something about safety in the Craftsmen Potters' Shop, I retorted not very politely, answering that nobody is going to lick my lion's tail which she accepted with a faint smile . . . At the School the price of the ingredients did not matter but in time the large amount of tin became exorbitant and the quality of the materials unreliable. As a matter of curiosity I give the formula '60-40-20-10' Litharge-china stone-tin oxide-flint (very fine sieve).

The height of my figures was restricted by the kiln to just over 20 inches [51 cm]. As the depth was 27 inches [68.5 cm] it was possible to fire one taller lying prone – very awkward. A stoneware figure of St Florian for a new house in Stanmore was fired that way.

The same method of rolling out a thin layer of clay was used to press tiles of which I made nearly 50 low-relief patterns, adding later several double sized. For all my work in the later years I used red earthenware Fulham clay and made up my own glazes. The ability to translate the things I saw or imagined into the 'assembly' parts allowed me to work very fast – and often slapdash – but I enjoyed my work and independence enormously, even the most tedious necessary parts of it.

BACKGROUND

On the 9th of September 1949 – almost exactly a month after my 52nd birthday – I was demobilized. From being a member of the welcome Polish army living in London already nine years and being a British citizen I became an almost penniless refugee without a profession, trade or skill, and an unsolvable problem for the Labour Exchange. But that served me well; I went to St Martin's School of Art and enrolled in the modelling class of the elderly sculptor Walter Marsden. He understood my problem, left me entirely free and was prepared to help if needed. I have learned there a lot, made several largish plastercasts and was told by Marsden 'You ought to have been a sculptor'. He suggested I should go to the Central School to learn pottery methods and make small figures: little did he know that I am already making them at home. He was very helpful in getting me a one year scholarship which was extended for another year. I never worked so much in my life as in the two years at the Central School of Arts and Crafts under Dora Billington.

A descendant of four generations of painters I was always interested in art and knowledgeable but never did anything in that direction. Towards the end of the war I saw in the magazine *Studio* an article about the terracottas of the sculptor Dobson: one of them made me want to try to copy it so I got some plasticine and tried. I don't know how

47 Bacchus – clay rolled out before basic shaping and assembly (Stanislas Reychan)

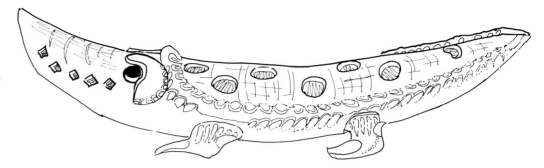

48 Crocodile, length 38 cm (15 in), flattened clay rolled round stick (Stanislas Reychan)

large the original figure was; I copied it from the photograph and it was very small indeed but I was surprised how easy it was. Gradually I tried more and more, using clay or substitutes. The late Alec Tiranti was very helpful. In the after-war gradual demobilization of the Polish Forces and the depressing results I decided to learn modelling properly. It seemed a crazy and irresponsible decision. [RDW's note: he had been ADC to the Chief of the General Staff of the Polish Army, receiving the MBE in 1944 'for services in the Allied Cause'. In 1946 the Army became the Polish Resettlement Corps, Stanislas then becoming Aide to the Inspector General.]

Already during my days at St Martin's I have made some figures at home, firing them at the Fulham Pottery – and tried to peddle them around the West End with promising results.

On a Sunday afternoon walk over Hampstead Heath I came across the Hampstead Open [-Air Show] and saw a woman selling pots. Asking if I may come the arrangers were not keen on pots but agreed to figures. So have started my exactly 30 years of gregarious and exhilarating summer weekends. It was glorious to meet customers, make friends (bad for ART?).

At the end of my time at the Central I was very lucky to move to a studio which I shared with Marion Morris, the Hungarian wife of a tax collector who made exquisite delicate figures: she had to leave after a year.

Intensely working all the time I have started as intensely to exhibit and find markets. At first to save electricity I used Fulham white clay with some slip colour and then transparent glaze, or T-material for a few unglazed stoneware figures like a pair of giraffes exhibited at the Royal Academy and sold there (a repeat pair was shown at the Salon de Paris and earned me a Bronze Medal in 1958, but they were damaged on the way home; a Silver one came in 1960). I had six figures at the Royal Academy and exhibited regularly at the shows of the National Society of Painters and Sculptors of which Society I became a member, being for many years in the Council and after 20 years an Honorary Member. The membership of the Red Rose Guild in Manchester and the Crafts Centre in Hay Hill followed and in Liverpool the Bluecoat Display Centre under the management of Elizabeth Zuckerman became for over 20 years one of my best

sales [outlets], with very friendly relations.

Regretably my relationship with the Craftsmen Potters Association of which I was one of the earliest members was not a very happy one. My figures and colours were a horror for the 'Stoneware Brigade' and I have undergone 'judgements' at special Council meetings. At one a young and apparently uneducated potter demanded that as a sculptor I should not be a member. At a second in which a venerable old woman took part whose lifetime work was making stoneware glazes from fruit tree ashes, she and another unfriendly member complained about a small ashtray of mine as too colourful. And years later I got to know that someone who managed the Shop deeply despised my work. But I did not resign and in the end was elected an Honorary Member; and I am very grateful to the CPA for my so very successful 'End-of-Work' exhibition in 1986.

JILL CROWLEY

Mermaid, stoneware (*Fig. 18*); *Hand*, raku (*Fig. 17*); study from life (*Fig. 49*)

DRAWINGS

The life drawings are made from moving models, frequently using stick ink on Chinese paper: they are about movement – drawing crystallizing thought. An existing interest in Chinese calligraphic art was further developed by seeing traditional methods in use during a visit to China itself that set off a series of thoughts leading to a more personal usage. Life drawing became an ongoing activity, moving away from intimidating academic exercise towards free experiment, already familiar in her handling of clay. The circus, juggling, and mime were fruitful sources; street performers could be hired as models by a group of artist friends.

A firm believer that everything you do affects everything else, she also believes that any worthwile breakthrough comes only as the result of a personal battle. Attending a life class was a way of ensuring a regular allocation of time, but when a need arose for something more substantial than paper with ink or charcoal she took rolled-out sheets of clay instead. Working freely with them direct from the model resulted in a series of wall-plaques, part drawn in pink porcelain inlay, part pushed out from the back or built up from the front, exhibited under the title *Ladies*. Made during pregnancy, they re-state the symbolic woman of pre-history.

MERMAIDS

Ideas abound, one grows from another. A figure drawing on clay had lines that looked rather like a tail – so she was off researching mermaids. She found a Victorian book about them, other information too on mermaids that had been kept in captivity. It was evident that there are many interpretations to explain what a mermaid is. Jill Crowley sees a middle-aged housewife mermaid with a family like her own, beset with the difficulties of underwater housekeeping, and feels sympathetic to her problems.

EXTRUDING

As well as using her own pug-mill for extruding small cylinders through a die, she has found larger diameters invaluable for students on short courses who are not experienced in handling clay: a good start is given without any need for skilled technique. Slab-rollers and arbitary press-moulded shapes can be used in the same way. She is surprised to find that extruding is still supplying her with ideas; it can be used far more flexibly than was apparent at first. As with all other ways of using clay, its response depends on condition: if just right, it can be persuaded to curve as it comes out of the pug-mill, but if too hard, it will buckle, and if too soft, it will collapse. It is necessary to be opportunist in making use of the shapes that present themselves. Many lengths are lined up and given the right sort of starting shapes by a nudge here and a thud there; likely ones are put away in a damp cupboard to be brought out gradually. At each stage she looks at them, considering possibilities, selecting some, rejecting others. Intuitive thinking is necessary all through; the ability to make the right choice develops with practice. One can learn only by experience.

The larger mermaids are constructed from sheets of clay rolled out, then wrapped around any suitably-sized cylinder. She has become adept at judging just the right point to remove the cylinder so that the clay slumps into mermaids of its own accord.

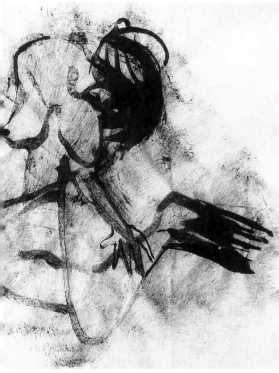

49 Study from life, model moving. On Chinese paper (Jill Crowley, 1988)

Jill Crowley herself feels that her way of working is closely related to the making of vessels; her exploitation of the natural tension of the material and manipulation of air in a sealed clay form belong to pottery rather than sculpture.

ARMS AND HANDS

Starting with an idea, she then tries out various ways of making and firing, using different colours and methods of decorating until the combination is found that best gives expression to the idea. There is always a surprise element, given by approaching from a different angle that might not have occurred to others. A single idea can be given many interpretations by playing around with the proportions, as in her series of arms and hands. Curved extrusions suggested arms, onto which hands could be modelled; there were large arms with small hands and small arms with large hands. This is intended as emphasis rather than exaggeration; if the hands are dominant it is because her interest was centred on them – as a writer concentrates on certain aspects of a text. This series originated in her delight in her small daughter's hands – tiny, like jelly, with no knuckles but incredibly expressive, continually moving in a way quite different from those of an adult. If you are acutely interested you notice more than usual; hands are everyone's most expressive feature after the face and eyes.

CATS

Juxtaposition of the unrelated often produces objects of unexpected power; such were Jill Crowley's series of raku cats' heads on smoked black plinths, which originated as externalizations of two unconnected causes of frustration, one domestic, one professional.

A bully tomcat had marked her kitten down for victimization. Coming silently into the kitchen by keeping the end of his tail in the catflap, he would stretch out to steal the kitten's food, then turn and bang the flap defiantly on his way out – only to leave an unmistakeable stink all the way down the path. Setting out for her studio, she discovered that he had even sprayed his tomcat smell on her leather coat. Furiously, she made hideous cat's head effigies to exorcize his evil influence. At the same time, a gallery showing her work had seemed to be attaching excessive significance to presentation on display stands, good pieces being excluded if no stands were free. For each head she therefore made an integral private plinth from sheets of clay pressed onto corrugated cardboard, fired and smoked. Tomcat and plinth, thus set apart and distanced from her by their own inviolable space for display, came to stand both for the exorcism of evil and for our need to preserve the inward spaces of our minds free from invasion or infringement.

RDW

MO JUPP

Standing Woman (Fig. 19); Doll (Fig. 20); Working drawings (Fig. 50)

Over the past 25 years I have tried to solve certain artistic problems, most but not all of my own making. My choice of materials, fired clay, has bewildered many of my friends in the 'business'. I have been at pains to point out that the fragility of clay is far outweighed by its speed of construction and its total indestructability. The possibilities offered by fired clay are so limitless that they allow me to see to the horizon. If I have inadvertantly pushed the parameters of ceramic acceptance to the limit, all to the good. In a word, fired clay gives me 'everything', a thought shared by domestic potters and hobbyists alike.

There are a number of fundamentals at risk:
1) I think a potter encloses space – a sculptor occupies it.
2) Most Ceramic Sculpture (?) is domestic, i.e. to be appreciated in the home, but very few concern themselves with the outside – the OPEN SPACE!!
3) Every artist should make FUNCTIONAL pieces. (This is confusing until you realize some fairly basic truths. No painter worth his salt first starts a painting like a doodle. He has an objective. Therefore the painting becomes functional!!) The main problem surrounding pottery or ceramics is that it could have two functions: 1) domestic function – casseroles, plates, soup sets, etc; 2) the other is much more difficult to examine . . .

I am often informed by my students that the mess in front of them is sculptural! When asked what they intended they become evasive. IT WILL NOT DO! AND DOES NOT. If an object has no use – *it is by definition useless, and should be thrown in the BIN.* This may sound rather domineering but logic must be upheld, harsh as it may sound. Most artists set out to accomplish certain things. They may die in trying but they must try!!! How many ceramic sculptors are prepared for this? Are they prepared to explain their motives? Should they? Or is this just the afterburn of things American? I speak as a teacher in this area and always insist that *my* students at least try to formalize what they want – how else can I help them? Artistically there is no such thing as a DISREPUTABLE idea – just an idea. SALES are nothing to do with anything. They help financially but VAN GOGH should be reinstated as the HERO of the new order. I understand the draw of Hockney but he doesn't allow for failure financially. This is an area the young find difficult to come to terms with – their being Mrs Thatcher's Young Britons!

Possibly these ramblings may sound nothing to do with what I make! But so to me. *The Helmets* were a discussion about the VULNERABILITY of man on the edge of existence – maybe man at WAR, man at war with the elements or danger. The *Temples* were a potential declaration of intent male or female. They were very explicit and there are many areas that were very introvert but they were what they appeared to be. *I am yours and this says it!!* The pieces with the bags on their heads were to do with how the young man sees women (a very dodgy area). He sees her – within male company – as a sort

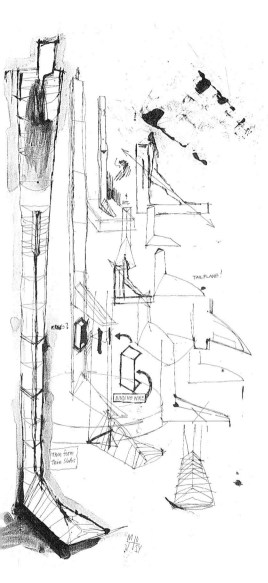

of threat. I wanted to overlay his fears with the way I (at 50) saw woman. Hence the page 3 woman with a target over her heart. He wanted what *all* men wanted but over everything he wanted someone to love him. I tried to make a 3D figure of all the nasty little witticisms of men, i.e. DOLL: BIRD: DOG: etc, but to always overlay the image with my own thoughts on the matter. (The people that own the pieces tell me that they provoke the most amazing comments.) The *Shields* were a comment on women using themselves as shields. Standing between the children and their potentially dangerous partners – something that most women have experienced in their lives as MOTHERS.

[RDW's note: Mo Jupp states that he is, at this point in time, too close to the making of his 2 m (6 ft) female figures to discuss them.]

50 Drawings for thinking through problems/ possibilities (Mo Jupp)

8 BIRDS – OTHER APPROACHES

TERRY BELL-HUGHES

Blackbirds Preening (Fig. 21); drawings – Dog (Fig. 51); Courting Bird (Fig. 52)

Why I should want to make figures or animals is a mystery, but perhaps it is because I do not understand myself or them; there is a certain awe inspired by our potency. Clay almost 'wills' me to make such things from it. A face – two holes for eyes, a nose stuck on, a cut for a mouth – it's as simple and as complex as that.

With clay, you can squeeze it, roll it, push it, wrap it around, press it, score it, impress into it, thumb it – build it into smallish shapes – handbuild figures and animals; sometimes they just 'happen' simply (that's marvellous), other times more preconceived, laborious, and other times again they do not work at all. All the time the clay reveals its nature and eggs you on, its changing character educating, from sticky to dry-hard, as it is spread, folded or broken, teaching a curious kind of muddy vocabulary that will eventually describe a shape.

I have no single technique of making, except rolling clay out with a rolling pin to a manageable thickness (say 8 mm [$\frac{5}{16}$ in]). Sometimes the clay is used sticky, sometimes harder. It is then scored or combed, or impressed, or rolled into crushed dry clays or sands etc, so that its surface cracks or changes. I then tear or cut pieces and start to build. Stiff clay is scored and slurried for joining pieces, soft clay is pinched or beaten for joining. Often clay is wrapped around or pressed into ready-made shapes, i.e rolling pin or bowl, occasionally altered (by cutting or beating) then allowed to stiffen and built upon further, adding torn pieces edge to edge for hollowness or cutting slabs for solidity. The shapes are often at the verge of collapse and the way of making directs the eventual sense of them.

I try to make fairly quickly, working on two or three at the same time, adding pieces of clay where they fit best, sometimes pinching from one to add to another. Concentration has to be complete and it is quite tiring, so that in a day four or five small shapes will be finished. I do take breaks, I go for a walk in the local woods or along the street, just to look at other things, away from the clay.

The pieces are dried over a few days and are then fired to high temperature (1280–1300°C [2336–2372°F]) usually reduced. Occasionally they are sprayed with ash or woodash and oxide, or salt and fired 'raw'. More often they are bisque fired (1000°C) [1832°F]), then oxide or glazes are put on, perhaps washed off or whatever process the piece seems to need to help its character. Some are spoiled at this stage.

I have few preconceptions other than a basic shape, so that drawing is sometimes irrelevant, but I do have a store of animal 'gestures' in my head, which come out as drawings with clay in mind. They are usually the less dignified postures of animals or sometimes people, such as birds preening, washing, squabbling, or sunbathing, or a man staring at himself in the moon.

I once came across a colony of cormorants on cliffs in North Wales. On several precarious levels, stubbled chicks with bald blind heads, stretched up their cavernous waving beaks. Their black parents rose and fell awkwardly on the air rising hundreds of feet from the sea. There was not much panic among them, more a close enquiry, requesting some explanation for my presence, my absurdity. There was noise and fear, hunger and motion. I was challenged in several ways, later I was very amused, and now some gestures remain.

To restate something of that animal 'presence', expression with words or marks on paper, or with bits of clay put together, are ways of attempting to convey it. For me, with clay, some absurdity persists, and finally expression is as much about the nature of clay as it is about anything else.

Clay: $\frac{1}{2}$ Crank mix $+ \frac{1}{2}$ St Thomas' Body (Potclays).

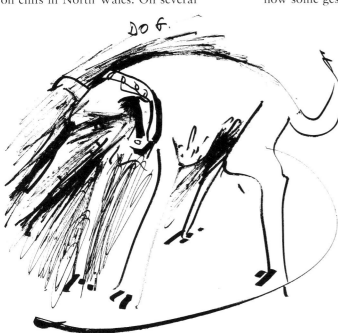

51 Dog – drawing with clay in mind (Terry Bell-Hughes)

52 Courting Bird – a less dignified posture remembered (Terry Bell-Hughes)

CLIVE BOWEN

Owl (Fig. 57); drawings (Heraklion Museum – Figs. 53–56)

Having children who are encouraged to come into the workshop it was inevitable that I should start making small animals for them. Often these are just quickly modelled bird and fish forms a couple of inches across, taking no more than a minute to make with incised detail. I then started to make thrown fish forms, again quickly made and biscuit-fired so that Jo, aged 5, could decorate them with brightly coloured poster paints.

A visit to Heraklion Museum was a great source of inspiration, not just because of the huge burial caskets but also for the delightful and unexpected thrown bulls' heads and various bird forms. Later a visit to the Picasso Museum in Paris and meeting the Japanese potter Taja Tajima-Simpson were both encouragements to continue to explore animal forms in thrown clay. Picasso's owl in particular was irresistible material to try to copy, and my daughter's obsession with horses gave rise to the latter-day Shebbear Pottery Tang Horse.

Above all animal forms are and always have been, I suspect, a source of pure fun

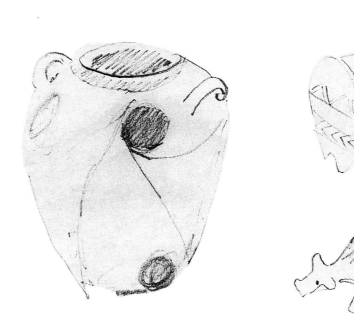

53–6 Bull and bird vessels with handles, cow with lid all thrown. Heraklion Museum, Crete (Clive Bowen)

and enjoyment for the thrower and a challenge to impart the immediacy of the throwing process of the clay into the animal form itself. The vagaries of the wood-fired kiln enhance this liveliness in the finished animal.

57 Owl, thrown and assembled after Picasso. Red North Devon earthenware clay (Clive Bowen)

NEIL IONS

Owl ocarina, (*Fig. 58*)

During my first few years of ocarina making, each bird or animal was entirely hand-modelled. As time went by and designs were elaborated I was spending more and more time on these smaller pieces of my range so I decided to rationalize the process a little.

I made a few moulds representing the basic families of bird species (e.g. wader, duck) in order to start the process from a basic press-moulded form. The two-piece plaster of Paris mould contains the form of the head and body pertaining to the type of bird, without beak, wings, tail, or legs. This allows for improvisation as to the species by changing the length of the neck, and deciding on the size and shape of the tail. The individual pose is achieved by the tilt of the head and neck, and the wing position. Therefore the process is simplified a little whilst still satisfying my desire for individuality.

The form is taken from the mould, the neck and head removed with a wire, and the body is fettled. It is at this point that I decide which species I am going to make. The neck is lengthened or shortened accordingly, the head joined at a specific angle or sometimes completely replaced with a pinched shape if the species is significantly different in this respect. The tail is formed from thin slabs and constructed with a whistle mouthpiece.

It is at moments such as this that I have to juggle aesthetic considerations with the practical requirements of the ocarina. Just as with a teapot maker, I have to balance design and function. I enjoy working out this compromise between the ocarina and the particular bird I am depicting, and it extends to the painting stage where I have a battle between naturalism and stylization – a battle in which I hope both sides share the victory!

The tail is joined to the body and the resulting ocarina is checked for sound quality. I apply thin slabs for the wings which are drawn out directly onto the clay and cut to shape before fixing – I do not use templates. The wings are merged with the body form and the bird is refined mainly by scraping with a junior hacksaw blade. Finally, if it is to be a standing bird, either a cone-shaped base or a branch is added onto which the legs are part modelled, part painted.

As ocarinas go my birds are fairly large. This scale was chosen because it fits the hand well, indeed my ocarinas nestle in the hand like a thrush-sized bird and this has an obvious appeal. Also the size gives ample scope for paintwork. The sound from these ocarinas is deep, mellow and gentle on the ear, another good reason for keeping to this scale. However, smaller ocarinas are included in my larger sculptural pieces, as with my grebes, which have small chick ocarinas riding on the adult's back. These are higher in pitch and louder – sufficient to attract mum's attention should they stray!

As soon as possible after modelling the piece is painted with earthenware slips. Areas are painted with two or three coats of various background colours. This is done following a definite procedure, starting with the base and underside of the bird, followed by the tail and the inside of the wings where they are exposed. The upper surfaces are painted with the bird on a bench whirler so as to minimize handling.

When the final background coat is touch dry, the pattern work/plumage is outlined with a dark-brown manganese slip, using a very fine lining brush. Detailed colour is painted within these delineated areas. Finally small details, particularly in dark colours, are applied in a more gestural/brushstroke manner over the main colour areas.

The position of the finger holes on the ocarinas is chosen for comfort and security in holding, so I usually just hold the bird and mark where the fingers fall. This is affected, however, by the modelling of the wings and occasionally the position of the head and beak – another compromise which sometimes leads to innovation. With respect to painting, the finger holes often form focal points for brush work and are sometimes used as starting points in the outlining of the design.

Originally inspired by American Indian ceramics, my work has moved gradually towards naturalism, followed by a brief period of re-assessment, and I hope now that it blends its derivation and my interpretation in fairly equal measure.
[RDW's note: 'Ocarina: a fluty bird-shaped musical toy, originally of terracotta.' Chambers Dictionary.]

58 Owl ocarina, height 20 cm (8 in). Basic press-moulded form with individual additions, painted with earthenware slips (Neil Ions)

JEREMY JAMES

Turkeycock (Fig. 22); drawings (Fig. 59)

I see myself very much as a sculptor working within the ceramic medium. Ideas, motivation, and sources are often extremely wide and diverse and as a result the techniques and materials that I use vary equally.

Sources to ideas that have initiated sculptures in the past have stemmed from such things as 2.5 × 4 cm (1 × 1½ in) newspaper cuttings to watching a particular animal's mannerisms. Drawing is nearly always the next step with sketch book work acting as an information gatherer as well as a design process. For myself at least, and I suspect for many other ceramicists, the transition from paper to clay is not always direct. Drawing, clay work, more drawing and so on is often the way I will solve a particular aesthetic or technical problem, such as which process and firing temperature are most suited to a certain idea.

The full, smooth forms of some large black pigs I have made recently, for instance, were very suitable for slip-casting. They were first modelled solid onto an armature and cast as a plaster mould. I've found for these that slip-casting works particularly well with the process of raku. The even quality of thickness I believe keeps loss from thermal shock very low; the slip is made from a white earthenware powder clay. They are bisqued to 1100°C (2012°F) and a very simple alkaline glaze is used.

Cockerels, birds of prey, and the turkey cock illustrated all require a different approach. The body of the bird is coiled or press-moulded, each one being adapted in various ways. The elegant layering of feathering I decided to build up from small elements, feathers in clay being worked separately using handcut plaster stamps, then individually applied. Slips, often vitreous, are the largest source of colour, glaze being used only sparingly just to give substance in some areas. Generally I do not like a glossy surface and find that glazes can cover up surface modelling or at the very least take a certain sharpness away. The work is gas fired in a reduction atmosphere to 1180°C (2156°F). Quite often there are further lustre and enamel firings to build up colour and surface.

I use plaster stamps quite extensively for feather patterns, combs on cockerels, wood textures, and many more. The plaster is worked in one or more of three ways, firstly by cutting or carving into it, secondly by casting onto modelled clay or lastly by casting onto found objects. Another way of handbuilding that I use to make, for instance, my birds on towers, is by building up the form from small pieces of textured clay. The birds have to be very slight and the thickness of the clay tends to be 3–4 mm ($\frac{1}{8}-\frac{5}{32}$ in) maximum. This method of building does call for quite close control of the dampness of the clay – hard enough to support the next piece but not too hard to push out from the inside in order to alter the form and to join the next softer piece of clay. It also calls for quite balanced building. I start from the feet and gradually build up the hollow shell; and in the same way that a real bird needs to balance, so do these. And yes they have overbalanced, landing in heaps on

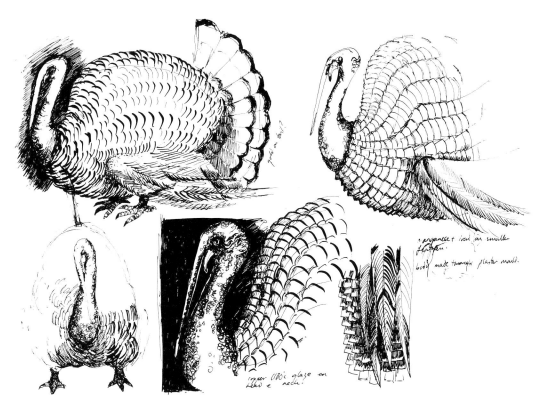

59 Exploratory drawings for turkeycock (Fig. 22) (Jeremy James)

the floor, usually at the end of a day's work!

As mentioned briefly before, motivation and ideas vary and I do not feel that I have any one continuous theme (except animals and birds perhaps). Broadly speaking the sculptures are celebrations and observations of animals. I am interested in the way we see animals, the pigs, for instance, originate from the nineteenth-century paintings of prize livestock. The commissioned painter was asked to accentuate the best points of the beasts and as a result you get these amazing paintings of huge cows and pigs with tiny legs and heads. I intend to do some more work around these paintings. I do not like animals sentimentalized or trivialized, their traditionally 'attractive' and 'repulsive' qualities being of equal fascination to me. The essence of a particular animal is always important to attain and it is *all* their aspects that make up their essence.

9 ANIMALS – OTHER APPROACHES

JENNIE HALE

Swan (*Fig. 60*); drawings from life – *Badgers* (*Fig. 61*); *Foxes* (*Fig. 62*); working sketches of foxes (*Fig. 63*); raku fox (*Fig. 64*)

DRAWING ANIMALS AND BIRDS

There are many reasons for the use of animals and birds as source material. They symbolize and express many emotions; the endless variation of form and colour constantly suggests new areas of interest – the deeper you go into the subject the more you see to lead you on and on. Studying them has been my lifelong passion.

Most of my drawings are made directly from living creatures, either in their own natural habitats or at zoos and wildlife parks; the foxes and the badgers illustrated were at a Field Study Centre. Museum specimens are also useful. I work quickly in pencil or ink to set down the forms and main characteristics, then a watercolour wash is applied, and finally detailing in ink.

Spending hours and days with an animal, drawing and painting, is fascinating – it is both a relaxation and a pleasure. With this close observation and patience, the subject is revealed in ways that give insight into behaviour and posture.

WORKING SKETCHES

From the life drawings a series of sketches develop, as a method of looking for forms that characterize the subject and bring out the aspects that interest me such as pattern, stance, form, humour – all of these play an important part in their development. Some just remain in the sketch book, others are looked at and additions made here and there from time to time, until a usable state is revealed.

These drawings are not intended as detailed studies for the finished piece but working sketches which show the essence of the subject. At times they develop alongside the clay work.

CONSTRUCTION IN CLAY

At present I am raku firing all my work, which makes special demands on the clay due to stresses in firing. I have now started using 'T' material which is incredibly strong and plastic. The forms are basically coiled, then altered in various ways with added detail.

The first section is built up fairly quickly to get a rough outline, then stretched, pushed, scraped, and thumbed together to tighten up the form. This stage is usually at about a third of the final height, or perhaps

60 Swan, length 48 cm (19 in). Raku with incised and waxed lines (Jennie Hale, 1988)

61 Badger cub, five months old, drawn from life (Jennie Hale)

62 Foxes, drawn from life at Dartmoor
Field Study Centre (Jennie Hale)

63 Working sketches of foxes, developing towards ceramically usable state (Jennie Hale)

at a point where there is a change of direction. The clay is then allowed to dry until about cheese-hard, when further coils are added; the form may then be completed or, depending on the complexity, may take a couple more stages of building and drying.

When it is in the right state, the whole piece is worked over by beating with a wooden paddle, then scraping with a kidney-shaped metal tool; finally a rubber kidney is used to compress the clay and smooth over the surface.

I now have the basic forms or 'dummies' which themselves suggest how they should be completed. The details are all added and drawn in whilst the clay is still cheese-hard, using balls, coils, slabs, and shaped blocks to make eyes, ears, beaks, feet and so on. This is done rapidly, using the modelling tool like a pencil cutting into the surface. Sometimes a pierced hole may be flared out to give nostrils, gapes, or a sunken eye socket.

COLOURING AND FIRING

When the form has dried completely, a selection of slips, underglazes, or stains are brushed onto the surface according to the individual item. This is mostly done before bisque firing, except for some which present problems.

The bisque firing is taken up to 1010°C (1850°F). After this wax resist may be applied before spraying with an alkaline frit glaze.

The glaze is fired in a 'top hat' raku kiln using bottled gas. It is made to my own design from an oil drum lined with ceramic fibre; there is a counterweight so that it can be lowered when the pieces are in place on the base, and safely lifted away when the firing is finished. The temperature is taken slowly to 600°C (1112°F), then quickly to 1000°C (1832°F), when the pieces are removed red-hot and buried in sawdust for about 20–30 minutes. When cold they are cleaned up with water and a scrubbing cloth; the waxed and incised lines hold the carbon, giving the quality of ink or pencil drawing, whilst the crackled glaze represents the texture of fur, feathers, or scales.

64 Raku fox, height 54 cm (21 in), resulting from studies and sketches (Jennie Hale, 1987)

TESSA FUCHS

Gorilla and Lady (Fig. 65); diagrams: *Gorilla and Lady*, and *Apple Tree (Figs. 66, 67)*

IDEAS, INFLUENCES, INSPIRATION

From earliest childhood I have had a great love and fascination for nature, trees, flowers, birds, animals, rocks, water, mountains, and landscape; the sky, the sun and moon, the seasons, the constant change. The wonder of the natural world always completely absorbs and delights me.

My other great passion is for painting – a world of pictures and colour.

When I was young I decided my vocation was to be a painter, but during my first year at art school I discovered clay. To be able to form anything one likes out of such a plastic and malleable material and then to be able to fire it and achieve such varied and colourful effects with glazes opened a new future for me.

When I left art school I set up my own studio making mainly practical ware which sold more easily in the late fifties and early sixties. As the years passed I turned to making bowls decorated with pictures and ceramic sculpture, the ideas coming from my own personal experience and love of nature and painting.

THROWING AS A BASIS FOR MODELLING

My sculpture is made from a half-and-half mix of potclays standard red earthenware and B.I.S. standard red earthenware. I throw and turn the main parts of each piece. This makes an excellent strong but hollow basis to the shape – very curvaceous and full. I first make a working drawing; from this I decide which part to throw, coil, slab, and model.

GORILLA AND LADY

(1) Throw and turn bodies and heads. (2) Shape and model the thrown bodies and heads while they are soft leather-hard. (3) Lie the bodies on their backs on a coil of soft clay for support and attach partly rolled, partly modelled legs with slurry; these are slightly hollowed. Leave to firm. (4) Turn the gorilla onto his feet and coil the neck. Leave to firm and then add the head. (5) Model in all the final detail – eyes, mouth, nose, toes, etc. Sponge over. (6) Take the lady and sit her on the gorilla. Make a good fit. (7) Attach the neck and part-rolled and part-modelled arms. Leave to firm slightly. (8) Model into the lady the fine details, then attach the hair made from tiny flattened curled coils, using slurry. (9) Leave to dry on the gorilla but remove for firing. (10) Always make sure there is no air trapped in any part.

FIRING

Kiln is electric, by Kilns and Furnaces – 61 × 61 × 61 cm (24 × 24 × 24 in). Biscuit firing: to 980°C (1796°F), taking two days. Warm up for 24 hours with bung open and kiln door ajar (but see note below). Sunvic 3 setting. Shut the kiln door and fire slowly

65 Gorilla and Lady. Earthenware thrown, coiled and modelled (Tessa Fuchs)

over the next 24 hours to 980°C (1796°F). Glaze firing: 1075°C (1967°F), taking eight hours approx.

[RDW's note: In normal workshop practice most potters take risks because they know that no one else is involved. If anyone touches the elements of an electric kiln when the power is switched on they will of course suffer severe burns and probable electrocution. For this reason safety devices are nowadays fitted to switch off the power when the door is opened. A drying cupboard – as suggested in chapter 3 – avoids the problem.]

GLAZING

MY BASIC GLAZE RECIPE (matt white)

Lead sesquisilicate	47
Whiting	10
Felspar	25
China clay	16

I use my basic glaze for all my ceramic sculpture, coloured with from 2 to 10 per cent of glaze stain or oxides. I also spray or paint thin layers of oxide under the glaze for a background colour. This gives me a complete range of colours and tones. I use a variety of techniques and build up the effect with layers of oxides and unstained and stained glazes. I pour, dip, paint, and spray the glaze according to the particular piece.

GLAZING THE GORILLA AND LADY

(1) Spray the gorilla with black glaze – 4 per cent manganese, 1 per cent cobalt in the basic glaze. (2) Spray over the legs and back of the neck with unstained matt white glaze (gives furry effect). (3) Clean out the eyes and inlay translucent brown glaze. (4) Dip lady in pale peach stained glaze. (5) Spray hair with bright yellow stained glaze. (6) Clean out eyes, inlay blue glaze.

Fire the two pieces separately. Fix together afterwards.

APPLE TREE

(1) Throw and turn trunk and apples. (2) Attach the roots with slurry to reversed thrown trunk. (3) Attach tapering rolled branches to the trunk with slurry. (4) When the tree is leather-hard sgraffito the bark texture. (5) Add the thrown apples with slurry and a small pellet of clay. (6) Add the leaves, cut individually from a thin slab, using slurry. (7) Sponge and leave to dry.

IN CONCLUSION

I am easily frightened and disturbed by the problems of the overcrowded and polluted world – a place of such extraordinary beauty but so badly threatened. I therefore create in ceramics a fantasy or myth – another world for myself, a place where creatures can fly, animals and men can live together in a state of friendship, love and humour (the *Gorilla and Lady*) where everything is larger than life in character, where my winged creatures can fly to a place of safety and sanctuary.

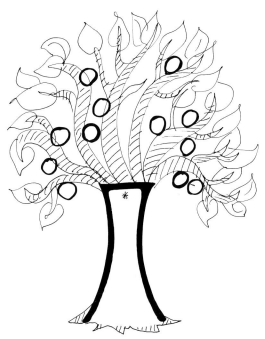

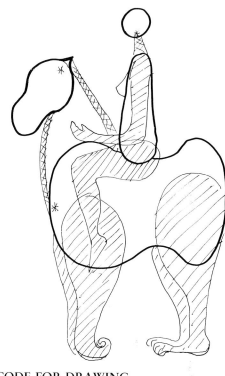

66, 67 *Construction diagrams – Apple Tree, Gorilla and Lady (Tessa Fuchs)*

CODE FOR DRAWING

◇ *THROWN AND TURNED*

▩ *COILED*

▨ *MODELLED*

◇ *SLABBED*

✳ *BASE OF THROWN SHAPE*

ALAN HEAPS

A Cat between Palm Trees (Fig. 68); drawings (Fig. 70); detail (Fig. 69)

Time and again, when I see several of my pieces together, I am forcefully reminded of the number of different ways in which I have used this one material, clay, and I appreciate even more our good fortune in having available this wonderfully versatile medium.

Clay allows me to build structures from flat slabs of harder clay, to construct bowls and animals' bodies by pinching it into shape and to squeeze it into a knife edge or roll it into coils. It can be cut, pierced, and bent or torn and broken to reveal its own texture, and I also make use of its capacity to take on the impression of other textured materials. It can be smoothed into soft, rounded forms or cut or beaten into sharp-edged structures. These are some of the ways in which I use clay but, of course, others choose to work with it differently, such as by throwing or slip-casting, for instance.

As technique is dictated largely by the type of body used, I have found I am generally most comfortable with Potclays St Pauls 1129, at least at the moment.

I use a small range of tools and equipment with which I have become very familiar. With a wooden rolling pin I roll out on a piece of chipboard, using slats of wood to raise the pin to the required height above the board when I am slab-making. Part of a hack-saw blade ground into a knife-shape is used for cutting, scraping, and modelling, whilst dividers are used for measuring and for drawing circles. I use a surform blade as a woodworker would use a plane for smoothing flat areas, and sometimes use twist-drills for making holes. The slats mentioned earlier come into use again for beating forms round or flat and for knocking joints tightly together. They also get used for stirring glazes and slips! I assemble my work on a board which is placed on a banding wheel so I can continually see it in the round.

My structures often require large slabs or smaller added pieces of varying thicknesses, and St Pauls copes well without cracking or warping during drying, which is done slowly under loose polythene sheets. It lends itself well to delicate modelling and, whilst containing a certain amount of grog, is still quite plastic.

Ideally, the day before use, I roll out perhaps a dozen suitable sheets of clay and cover them with a polythene sheet to bring them all to the same wetness. I might use a paper template for complicated symmetrical shapes, and the parts are joined with slip, the joints being beaten together and cross-hatched deeply with a knife and then smoothed over. After the main structure is complete, smaller shapes are added and then any modelling, using the tools mentioned before and, of course, my fingers. Most structures need internal ribs to give them strength. As my electric kiln is small, that is 0.05 cu. m (2 cu. ft), larger pieces are designed in such a way as to be made in sections, fired separately and assembled later. My ceramics take anything up to 40 hours each to build.

As I am working with the clay I am inevitably bearing the glazing in mind. After bisque firing to 900°C (1652°F) I paint and spray with mixtures of slips and glaze stains.

I might incorporate wax resist either before or after this. I either dip or pour when I am glazing and my glaze is matt, off-white and lead-based, fired to 1110°C (2084°F). After glazing and before firing, I often spray on a mixture of the glaze and glaze stains. Being a dry glaze, this never runs so there is no need to use batt wash; however, I sprinkle grog on the batts, which I think helps the pieces to shrink without trauma.

My pots seem to come about in two ways. One is through ongoing development from previous pieces and the other is a continual source of surprise, that is, when new unthought-of pots appear in my mind, seemingly from nowhere. Either way, I make drawings which form the basis of what I am about to make. These drawings have to stimulate me visually and this inevitably leads to a feeling of enthusiasm as I see the different roads I might take, choices which continually present themselves throughout the making of each piece.

The arts and architecture of earlier cultures are of great interest to me, as are plants, animals, and mechanical works, interests which are often reflected in my ceramics.

In this illustration of *A Cat between Palm Trees*, the large structure is a doorway derived from a combination of Indian and South American architecture. I first used this form several years ago as an entrance to a Village. The interests I have mentioned are clearly reflected in this piece in that the palm

68 *A Cat between Palm Trees. Constructed from cut-out rolled shapes with added modelling. Earthenware (Alan Heaps)*

69 *Detail of A Cat between Palm Trees (Alan Heaps)*

trees can be recognized as aloes from my large collection of plants, the snakes and frogs inhabit my garden, and I have several cats. A future departure might be made from one small part, say the moon carrying his own night-sky.

Although I am not conscious of my work developing and have no idea of what it will be like in the future, I see much greater breadth in it than even ten years ago, though during the ten years I have made several thousand pieces.

70 *Exploratory drawings for visual stimulus, relating to A Cat Between Palm Trees (Alan Heaps)*

PETER M. CROTTY

Cat (Fig. 1)

Practical pottery making is something I had not considered until I met Rosemary Wren in 1970. Friends had told me that throwing was difficult . . . and that studio potters, restricted to 'safe Low-Sol glazes' (?) could never aspire to the heights of industry. These early views must have been modified by reading of Faber monographs, meeting Terry Bell-Hughes (q.v.), and visits to Marshall Street and numerous kitchen shops. But here I was faced with the tactile material itself.

From (inevitable?) raku-esque tea-bowls I moved on to animals, people, and boats. Now it seems that I had never been short of ideas, nor of some sense of pattern. What fascinated me about clay was the ease with which it could be put together – unlike wood or metal. To make an aesthetically and technically viable boat in wood is a very difficult undertaking, with other people's standards to be met – but clay planks can be shaped almost without thinking and nailed or seamed together . . . with just clay. Cats, as in Fig 1, curiously enough, could be made in the same carpentering manner. It is

necessary to think 'Cat', and make. Sometimes the thing made does not say 'cat' back to you – or anything else – in which case it can be scrapped or, better still, cut or broken into pieces to make building blocks for a further attempt. Terry Bell-Hughes' 'Clay Way' of looking at the material for what it can tell you is an essential part of the technique. One is, as it were, selecting from a kaleidoscopic infinitude of possible shapes the one that will fit or follow on from what is to hand. A key to what will fit can be found in the concept of metamorphosis. If a shape can suggest something other than its obvious self, bring in some further allusive cross-reference, then so much the better.

The clay must not be chewed or mangled – ways must be found to maintain freshness and tension. I make much use of clay turned inside out, pinched tubes, or sheet. Decoration should follow form. I have always felt that if you can make it, you should be able to paint it, though for all that a sometimes cage-cup complexity of shape was more daunting than the cartridge and

gouache I had been used to for some years.

Creatures, boats, and men should all cry out. Recently, a student challenged me on this – 'Why do you want to call attention to the horrible in life?' I don't, but the *rasa* I would inbuild or wish to come out will not be *śānta* (peace) as in Rosemary's work, but rather *adbhūta*, (wonder), *bhayānaka* (terror), *karuṇa*, (compassion – in or for the onlooker?), or often *hāsya* (ribald laughter).

A quality I appreciate in others' work is wit. A quality I would like to bring out in my own work is a greater simplicity of form and decoration . . . but without, however, losing the richness of allusion ever present where 'Clay is words, and Words are clay'.

ANNA ADAMS

Genet (Fig. 71); drawings (Figs. 72 and 73)

I find it exciting to draw a moving target and I enjoy capturing the essential expression of animal bodies. In the beginning I thought it a good idea to make animal forms in order to record them before human beings destroyed the whole creation, but I must admit that this pessimism would not have sufficed as a main motive for making art. My true reason for concentrating on animals as a subject is that their mysterious otherness fascinates me. One may be attracted, initially, by sheer decorativeness, but soon one finds oneself seeing, or experiencing, a bird (or a toad or a bee) from within, and much empathy goes into the making of any of my creatures, from tigers to sheep. What can it be like to see the world through the watchful eye of a sitting blackbird, or from the sly centre of a foxy awareness?

Working in clay, with its native tendency to lie abed, one has to think of methods of construction that persuade the inert material to stand up and look alive, and the method has to be built into the design. Larger masses must be hollow because of clay's other

71 Genet from London Zoo. Curved bridge-like slabs of clay with coiled head and neck (Anna Adams)

grazing cow made from slabs

18 inches, approx.

Coiled rectangular body Turned on its side &
developed into a RAM in a THICKET.

72 Decorated rectangular animals made from slabs or coils (Anna Adams)

tendency – to explode in the kiln if solid – so to coil up forms as if they were primitive pots is one obvious solution. To make things of rolled-out slabs of clay, angled together, is another. I use both these techniques. To coil up natural forms it is necessary to be able to think in sections, and to construct things in slabs one must think in planes, or solid geometry. At one time I made a series of cows which were based on rectangular, boxlike shapes, like a herd of bovine sideboards. The vertical surfaces of these boxes came right down to the ground, to avoid the problem of breakable legs, and the bellies, udders, and legs of the cows were modelled in low relief. A farmer who lives nearby, seeing these cows, asked 'How do you milk them?' You don't, of course, but sometimes they had very low-relief milkmaids or suckling calves drawn on them.

I also decorated their plane surfaces, which resembled fields, with patterns of daisies or thistles.

At another time I made a number of larger-than-life-size nesting birds: blackbirds or thrushes in bushes, or grounded skylarks in grass. Some of the blackbirds were in hawthorn bushes, others in wild rose or honeysuckle thickets, for I painted flowers in an impasto of white clay onto the reddish or blackened bodies. The shapes of these were rounded and simple, so I used to coil up the basic form. I made several nesting blackbirds that I cut in two, so that the bird's head and back would lift off to reveal a cluster of nestlings inside. These too would lift out to show a clutch of blue or green eggs painted onto the bottom of the bowl.

Living, as we have for about 30 years, in rural Yorkshire, we used to keep bantam

Corbusier henhouses.

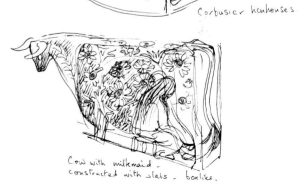

Cow with milkmaid
constructed with slabs - boxlike.

hens and other fowls on our croft, and these, in their day, furnished more ideas than eggs. I went through a phase of building sitting hens from triangular planes of clay, so that the result was like both a hen and a house, as hens are both mother and dwelling-place for a brood of chicks. In my mind I called these things 'Corbusier Hen-houses', but I didn't make such notions public.

The Genet jungle cat (*Fig. 71*) was made in 1987. Since 1986 I have been living for part of each year in London, and I am able to get to the zoo and draw exotic creatures once again. My *Genet*'s underlying structure consists of two curved slabs of clay, leaning together. I thought of it as a bridge, and even its spots seem to line up like courses of bricks. The tail is also made of sickle-shaped slabs of clay, but the head and neck are coiled.

I find that I have a run on a particular creature, and once I have spent the impetus given by an exprience – of drawing or simply observing – I cannot go on doing it for the sake of money. A large part of any creative work must be experimental; it inhibits development to be expected to repeat oneself too often, and this fact inhibits commerciality, which is unfortunate. The borderland between art and craft is a difficult terrain in which to make a living.

nesting bird – coiled like a pot.

coiled.

blackbird in a hawthornbush.

73 Coiled-pot nesting birds (Anna Adams)

10 EARNING YOUR LIVING

There is plenty of room at the top of the tree, as my mother used to say. To get there, however, inspiration must first be translated into reality through hard work and experience. Your own interest, and that of your public, must then be maintained continually by further challenges.

The magic of the market then begins to operate. You – inspired artist or artisan – have brought forth, and what price your children? A sparrow for two farthings? – but let us say £10. If this is your price you must find a buyer – try a shop or gallery. Now for the *hokkano baro* – the big trick. By wholesale discount your £10 becomes £6 or £7 . . . and sometimes in minutes, sometimes in months, the customer pays £16/£17. Your original creation has become raw material for resale. This pay-off you as creator can never achieve. Remember that unless you sell direct, you will, as primary producer, be always at the lowest end of the chain – certainly paid accordingly, possibly treated accordingly. But for all this abstract consideration, do not think that you can do without the support of a sympathetic retail outlet, entitled to a just profit.

To have reached this point you will by now have developed pride in doing the job well; genius consists of the ability to take an infinite amount of trouble. It can then take an effort to extend this to producing what you have promised at the expected time. A shop may well find it easier to deal with somebody reliable, rather than wait for brilliant work from an unreliable maker; explaining away your own lack of organization by pleading a 'sensitive artistic temperament' will not earn your living nor that of the shopkeeper.

Visitors to workshops and exhibitions very often misread our situation. 'How clever you are!' they say. 'How lucky to lead such a creative life and do just what you like all day! How relaxing it must be!' These comments are likely to be received in tactful silence, as the apparently laid-back creator is probably wondering whether the visitor's cheque will pay the electricity bill for the last firing, and knows that the rest of the day must be spent on composing introductory notes and organizing a publicity photograph for the next exhibition, writing invoices, and packing finished work to take to the Post Office. Then there are accounts that should have been sent off for tax purposes . . . and if no glaze tests are made up before tomorrow's firing, the ginger cats may well come out purple again the next time. All this is indeed made worthwhile by the comparatively short creative periods, but I hope it is clear by now that these are not just a matter of being clever.

There are also those who ask the price of clay and raise their eyebrows to think of the enormous profits we are making. This is far from the truth! Individual sculptural ceramics are very labour-intensive and the public sees only the tip of the iceberg. Few of us earn as much as a skilled garage mechanic, and we can be found working at all hours of the day and firing kilns well into the night. Face the situation before you start, and help your family or dependents to understand and appreciate your essential need to be free in spirit. Any compromise made with commercial intent results in loss of intrinsic value – so nothing is gained anyway. If your real interest is in making money, look elsewhere!

Traditionally, the craft of working in clay

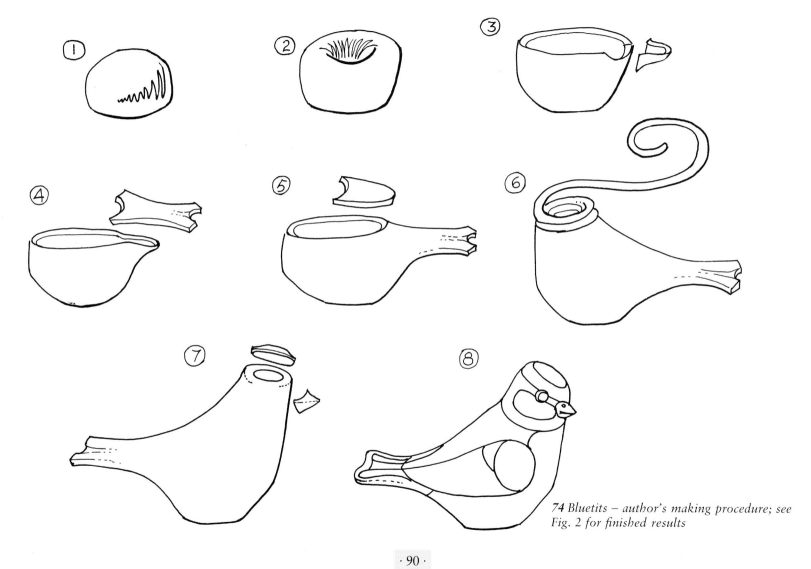

74 Bluetits – *author's making procedure; see* Fig. 2 *for finished results*

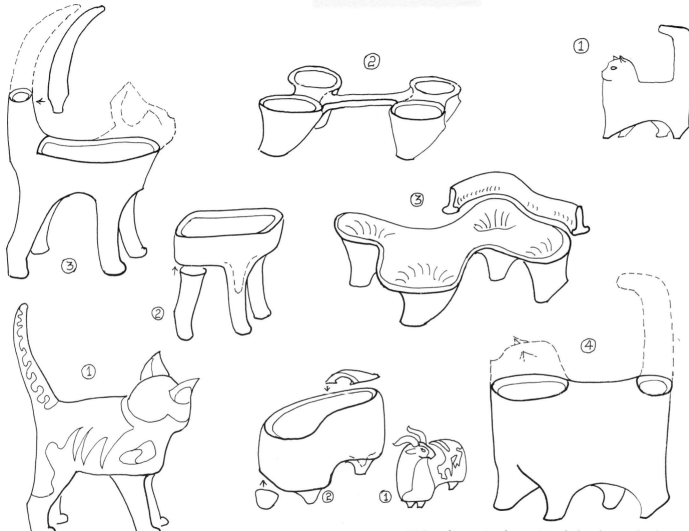

75 Standing animals – original sketches and solutions (see p. 92)

has always been the poor relation of the fine arts: they are made of bronze, stone, wood, or paint. The concept that works of art of equal merit can be made in clay is new. Fine art auctioneers and galleries have only just begun to give them equal treatment, but on the whole prices remain far lower. Art critics are wary, perhaps deterred by unfamiliar technicalities, so comment on exhibitions may well be relegated to the women's pages as being of lower status, of domestic interest only. Since about 1960, however, a considerable body of knowledgeable collectors has developed, of modest means but pioneering discernment, who have fostered the movement and made possible the earning of a modest living.

This situation seems to be much the same in other countries where the development of ceramics has been along the same lines. In Britain a very few 'sculptors using clay' have already broken through the fine art barrier; some of them are represented in this book and many others are following. One tells me that his sculptor friends wonder why he chooses to use such a strange medium as clay, another that her potter friends wonder why she 'wastes' so much time in life classes. We all make our own barriers!

My own way of earning my living came about through asking Ladi Kwali, maker of traditional Nigerian hand-built pots, how she had learnt. Her reply was that her mother had shown her that for a cooking pot you must make a certain series of movements with your hands, for a waterpot another series. Each time the result was different but acceptable for its purpose: the repetition was through the hands rather than the eyes. There was no copying of external appearances.

Thinking in this way – developing a procedure for each type of creature – I have found it possible to use my original drawings again and again, but each clay creature, like the Nigerian cooking pots, has a life of its own. There is no intention of making them the same or of making them different: each is an individual.

The bluetits in Fig. 2 are examples out of several hundreds made in the last ten years or so, kept because form or glaze was particularly good. The drawings in Fig. 74 have set out the making procedure; I never decide which way the head is to turn until it becomes inevitably dictated by the line flowing through body and tail. The problems that have already been solved – size, which glazes to use, how the pattern was stylized – are noted in a record book to save going over the same ground again; this is updated as new ideas arise. The original drawings for my cats and sheep (*Figs. 37 and 43*), with constructional solutions are shown in Fig. 75.

This way of working within a deliberate limitation has also made it possible to produce a list so that galleries and individuals can order specific creatures with some idea of what they are likely to receive: some 80 are now included. On display in our workshop is a collection of examples which are never sold, and a book of photographs numbered in accordance with the list. Ex-workshop prices are given, that is, the price that we expect a customer to pay at our studio. A 30 per cent discount off these prices is normal for galleries buying in quantity for resale; this discount is effectively the major part of one's advertising budget. Newcomers to the scene are sometimes shocked to find that this wholesale price will then be doubled (referred to as 'uplifted 100 per cent') by most galleries, with, in Britain, sales tax at 15 per cent added on top. You have to realize that it does take time and money to sell your work: either your time or that of the galleries who are better equipped for the purpose. The more reasonable do not object if some of their customers go direct to the makers on occasion.

Stimulating challenges are always worth taking up, however disconcerting they may be at first. The Australian black swans on the jacket front make a good example. A particular collector, who has work of ours made over many years, asked 'Have you ever made swans?'. Thinking of the faultless line of their superbly elegant necks and the many commercial parodies, I replied 'No – but why?'. 'I just wondered what you would make of them. Let me know if you do make any . . .'

Now this is just the right kind of challenge, for it left me free to find my own solution. One learns to be wary of people

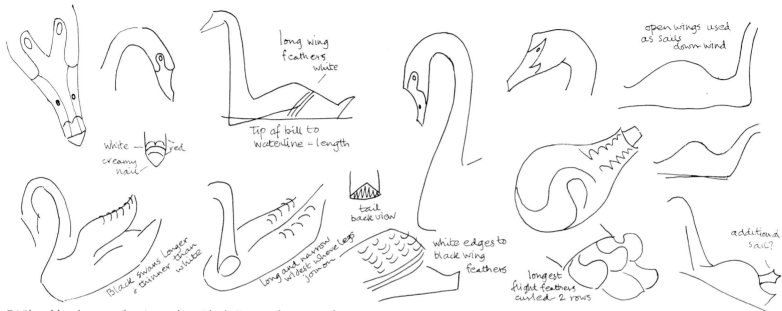

76 Sketchbook notes for Australian Black Swans shown on front cover

who know just what they want in every detail and expect you to make it. It took a year before I came across some swans not white (our white was then tending to flake off) but black; also the curve of their necks was quite different, more austere. Fig. 76 shows the sketchbook notes. Did he mind if they were black? No, that would be fine. Another six months (the black swans are about 32 km [20 miles] away) and I had more or less fathomed the complexities of their curly wing-feathers. But they really are

very large – yes, that was acceptable. The risk is inevitably ours – if not approved, they would have to go elsewhere, and one's next few weeks' finances do not always allow risk. Eventually a very reasonable ultimatum ('By Christmas, or the offer is withdrawn!') pushed me over the brink, the wing-feather problem solved itself, and the black swans now occupy an honorable position amongst a richly-varied collection.

This is the opposite end of the market to the bluetits – variety being the spice of life.

Exhibitions, too, present an opportunity to stretch one's abilities and see the work in a quite different context. Acquire a good camera for making a photographic record of your best work; write the date and size in pencil on the back, and keep them in readily-available form, with exhibition cards, press cuttings, and any other landmarks in your career. From time to time they will suddenly be needed, and you will have only yourself to blame if someone more publicity-minded than yourself steals the front cover again!

The days never seem long enough to complete everything intended; organization is needed to avoid frittering away time. Growing family responsibilities may mean less time to work, but parents discover that they can learn to work more intensively for shorter periods. Even small children, given a corner of their own and real tools, can work alongside their parents; their attention may soon wander but they are learning that art is a serious form of work.

It is necessary to learn how to manage one's own temperament, perhaps doing a routine job when creative energy is low; even depression can be used positively to initiate unpalatable change. Make sure that all arrangements with shops, galleries, and customers are clear – who is paying for what, and when? How many pieces are expected, have the price range and delivery date been discussed? Find out the comparative cost of the various methods of delivering your work, not forgetting insurance. There are several different types of both postal and rail service as well as direct deliveries; if you are using your own transport it is reasonable to make a charge too. Learn to pack your pieces firmly and safely – maybe you can find a source of re-usable materials. A sale or return basis is usual for exhibitions, but try to avoid it for normal stock as soon as you can: outright sale is the only means of knowing where you stand. Offer to exchange any pieces unsold by a gallery at the end of six months or a year; this will encourage them to take a risk and the piece may well fit in better elsewhere. The most successful gallery owners will appreciate your friendship as much as they enjoy your work, so if you see problems coming up over delivery dates, tell them – they are very used to this but need to plan ahead themselves.

Check your business procedure to avoid duplication of effort, and keep careful and precise accounts as you go along. Certain bills need paying at definite intervals and your production and cash flow must be regulated to fit. Find an accountant who is sympathetic to the self-employed; his advice is invaluable, and you will recoup his fees by not paying unnecessary taxes. Consider carefully the apparent advantages of prestigiously-advertised 'Craft' and 'Design' shows; how much would you need to sell to break even, when time lost and cost of travelling are added to expensive stall rental? Could you – and do you want to – cope if massive orders result?

Some grants and awards can be wonderfully helpful, but make sure what is expected of you in return. Commercially-orientated schemes are devised on the assumption that everyone wishes to expand, but if your ceramic sculpture is an expression of your personality nobody else can make it for you. Many potters work in couples or groups, sharing major equipment; one partner may not be an originator on the making side but can keep the books, prepare clay and glazes, pack and fire kilns, and send off finished work. Do not, however, let them dictate what you shall make; rather than compromise, be prepared to undertake occasional or part-time teaching, or perhaps fund your real work with some other quite separate ceramic production, more saleable but having its own integrity.

Lastly, join a potters' association and a mixed craft guild at any level that their selection committee sees fit; if this is not full membership at first, join as an associate and bide your time, for committees change in personnel and policy. Send in your work to their exhibitions – this was the first step for many now at the top. At their meetings you will find yourself part of a wide camaraderie ready to share your problems and joys, for they have all been through the mill themselves and understand the call of clay and fire.

SUPPLIERS

CLAY

Hyplas 64 in powder form is produced by English China Clays (ECC), John Keay House, St Austell, Cornwall, England. The minimum order that they will deliver direct is 10 tons. If collected personally or by a carrier from their works at Bovey Heathfield, South Devon, the minimum order is one ton – but contact St Austell first. ECC also export widely; contact St Austell for information on local suppliers.

Smaller quantities are not normally stocked by potters' suppliers except Whitfield and Son, 23 Albert Street, Newcastle-under-Lyme ST5 1JP, who will deliver anywhere in Britain.

'T' MATERIAL

Manufactured by Morganite Thermal Ceramics Ltd, Liverpool Road, Neston, South Wirral, Cheshire L64 3RE, England who will deliver quantities of one ton and over direct. Smaller quantities are available from most potters' suppliers. For overseas customers there is an extensive Morganite International presence through whom it could be obtained; contact the above address for details.

PORCELAIN BODY

'Audrey Blackman Porcelain', obtainable worldwide from Valentine Clay Products, The Sliphouse, Birches Head Road, Hanley, Stoke-on-Trent, Staffordshire ST1 6LH, telephone 0782 271200. This firm prepares specialized bodies to order and could supply the Hyplas 64/grog mixture in plastic form.

PERIODICALS

The most satisfactory way of locating current suppliers is through their advertisements in the ceramic periodicals. In Britain consult:
Ceramic Review, 21 Carnaby Street, London W1V 1PH, England.
The following are listed alphabetically by country:
La Revista del Caramista, Quirno Costa 1259, 1425 Buenos Aires, Argentina
Crafts Arts Magazine, P.O. Box 363, Neutral Bay Junction, NSW 2069 Australia
Pottery in Australia, 2/68 Alexander Street, Crows Nest, NSW 2065 Australia
La Ceramique Moderne, 22 rue Le Brun, 75013 Paris, France
La Revue de la Ceramique, 61 rue Marconi, 62880 Vendin-le-Vieil, France
Verlag Neue Keramik GmbH, unter den Eichen 90, D-1000 Berlin 45, Germany
Keramik Magazin, Steinfelder Strasse 10, D-8770 Lohr am Main, Germany
Keramiki Techni, P.O. Box 80653, 185 10 Piraeus, Greece
Keramiek, Pueldijk, 3646 AW Wavereen, Holland
Ceramica Italiana, Vir Firenze 276, 48018 Faenza 276, Italy
The New Zealand Potter, Box 147, Albany, Auckland, NZ
Ceramica, Paseo de las Acacias 9, Madrid 9, Spain
FORM magazine, Box 7404, S-103 91 Stockholm, Sweden
Studio Potter, Box 65, Goffstown, NH 03045, USA
Ceramics Monthly, P.O. Box 4548, 1609 Northwest Blvd. Columbus, Ohio 43212 USA

INDEX